1ST GRADE PHONICS
Unit 1
Phonograms 1–26

MW01593372

TABLE OF CONTENTS

IMPORTANT: Please refer to the Teacher Guide for specific scripts, procedures, and words that are represented by pictures.

Throughout this Unit, learners will scan QR codes. Be careful they scan each code individually.

LEARN

- Consonant and vowel sounds
- Lowercase letters
- Closed syllables

VOCABULARY

consonant sounds   closed syllable

vowel sounds   mutli-letter phonogram

phonograms

DAILY PAGE GOALS

Day	Complete	Day	Complete	Day	Complete
1	ii–iv	7	25	13	60–61
2	1–5	8	26–34	14	62–69
3	6–8	9	35–43	15	70–79
4	9–14	10	44–45	16	80–87
5	15–22	11	46–54	17	88–94
6	23–24	12	55–59	18	95–96

Teacher reads all pages to the Learners.

WELCOME

Meet your Piney Forest friends. They are going to help you learn.

Help Manny Turtle get to school!

1. WHAT IS PHONICS?

Learn:

- Understand how consonant and vowel sounds are different.
- Practice writing lines.

Vocabulary:

consonant sounds *[́kŏn sǐ nŭnt s<u>ou</u>ndz]* – sounds that are
    blocked or partly blocked by the tongue, teeth, or lips

vowel sounds *[́vow ŭl s<u>ou</u>ndz]* – sounds that are voiced and open

---

In Phonics, you will learn how to read and write. You will learn about letters and their sounds.

Point to and name the letters you know.

a b c d e f g h i

j k l m n o p q r

s t u v w x y z

WORKING WITH SOUNDS

When we read, we turn letters into sounds. **Vowel sounds** are voiced and open. That means we move our vocal cords and keep our mouths open.

Voiced

Open

 Circle the correct answer.

1) Who is making a vowel sound?

Consonant sounds are blocked or partly blocked. That means we move our teeth, tongue, or lips to block our breath. Consonant sounds may be voiced or unvoiced.

Blocked or Partly Blocked

Voiced or Unvoiced

ch, j, sh

w, qu

mmm

sh

Circle the correct answer.

2) Who is making a consonant sound?

WRITING

You should sit like this when you write. Put your feet flat on the floor. Keep your back straight. Lean forward.

? **Circle the correct answer.**

3) Who is sitting correctly?

Your paper and pencil should look like this. Slant your paper. Pinch your pencil between your thumb and pointer finger. Let the pencil rest on your middle finger.

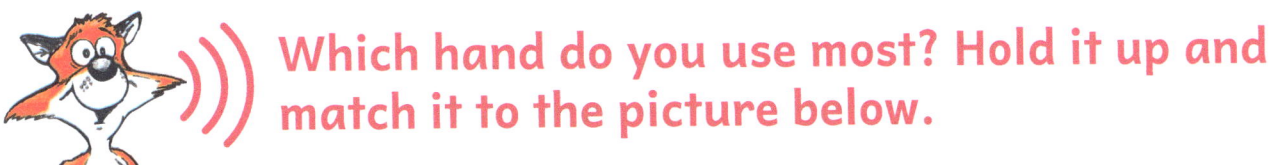

Which hand do you use most? Hold it up and match it to the picture below.

pencil grip

left   right

Circle the correct answer.

4) Which hand is holding the pencil correctly?

Check your writing position.

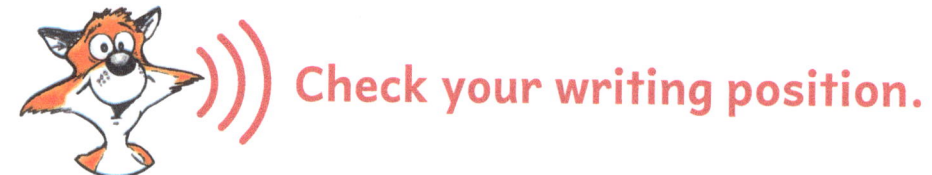

The 3 Ps of Penmanship

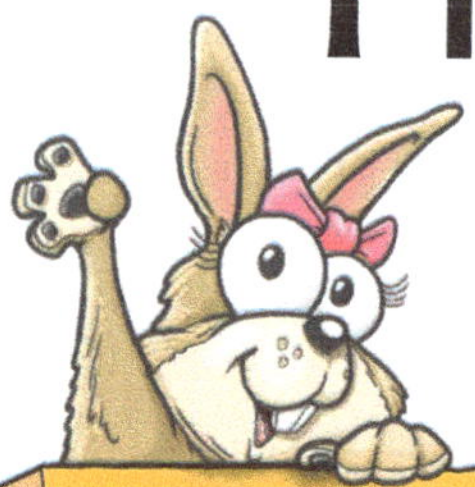

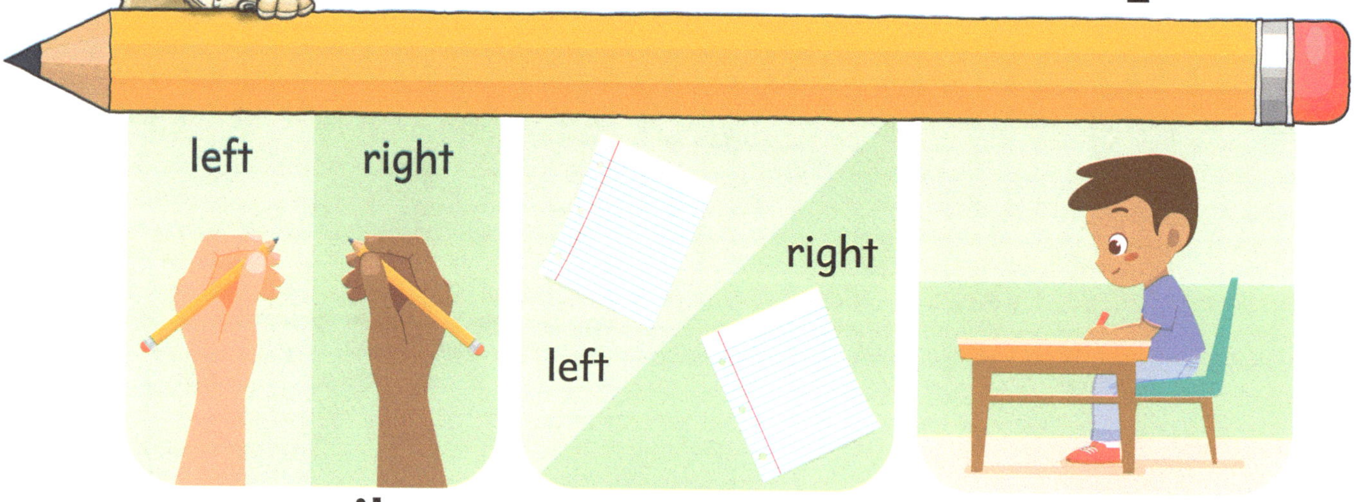

left
right
right
left

pencil **paper** **posture**

In this Unit, you will learn how to write lowercase letters. They are small letters. You will use these lines.

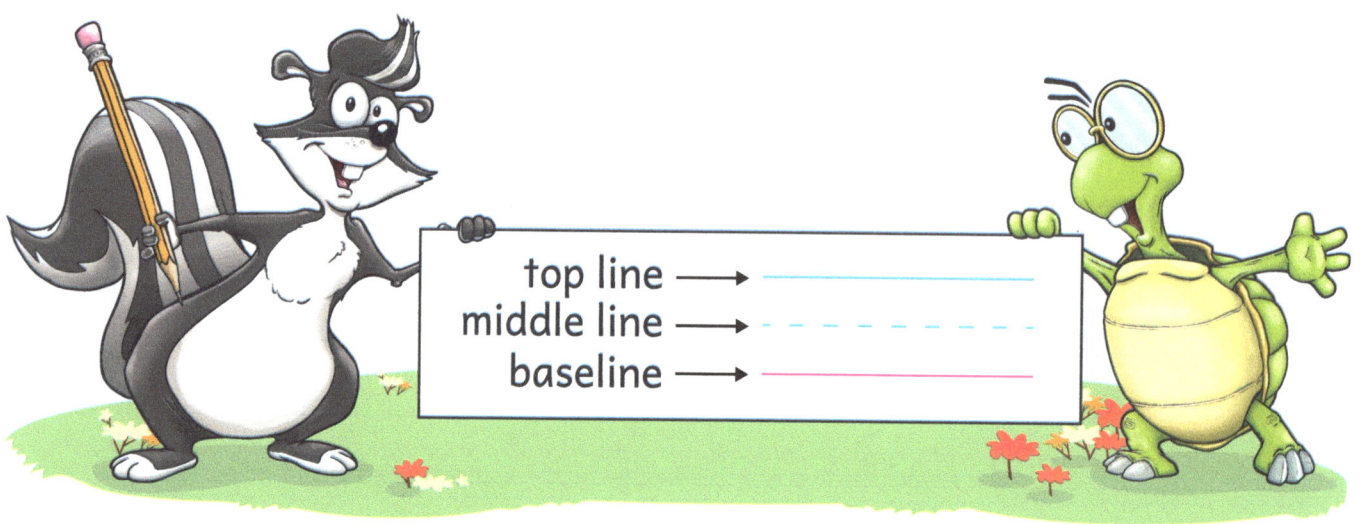

top line →
middle line →
baseline →

 **Trace and write the lines.**

5) Start at the top line. Pull down straight.

6) Start at the top line. Slant left.

7) Start at the middle line. Slide right.

8) Start at the base line. Push up straight.

Look at the numbers on this clock. We will use them for the spaces between lines.

 **Circle the correct answers.**

9) Where are numbers 2, 4, 8, and 10?

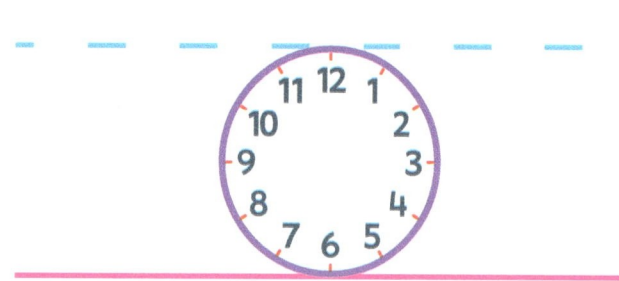

Write the correct answers.

10) Start at 2 o'clock. Circle back.

11) Start at 10 o'clock. Circle forward.

SCORE   CORRECT   RESCORE

Learn:

- Write and say the sounds for the letter **a**.
- Identify the short and long sounds of **a**.

Vocabulary:

phonograms [ˊfō nĭ grămz] – written letters that represent sounds

---

(((**Listen. Mark ⊠ when done.**

PHONOGRAMS

You will start learning phonograms. **Phonograms** are letters that represent sounds.

m**a**sk   st**a**ge   t**a**lk

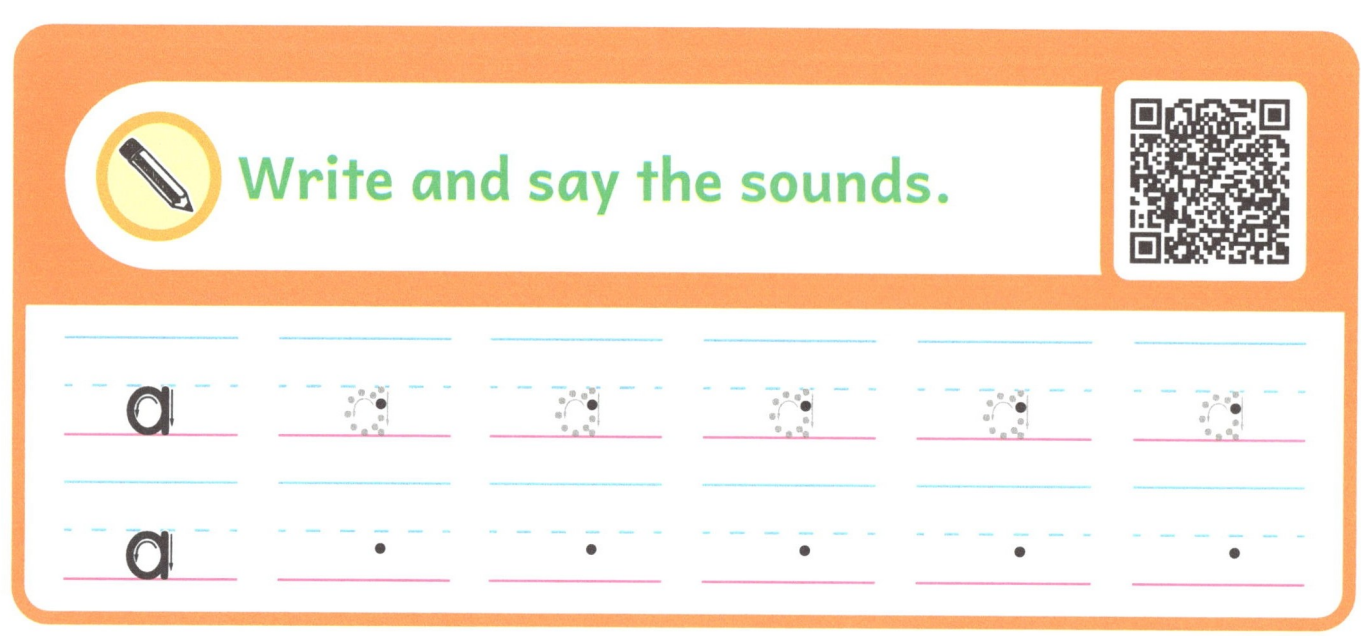

✏️ **Write and say the sounds.**

a

a

1ST SOUND OF a

All vowels make more than one sound. The first sound is its short vowel sound.

Listen to the words with short a.

Circle the correct answers.

1) Which TWO words have the short **a** sound?

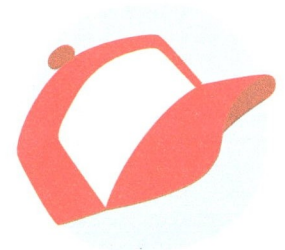   

2) Which TWO words have the short **a** sound?

2ND SOUND OF a

A vowel's second sound is its long vowel sound. It sounds like the letter's name.

 Listen to the words with long **a**.

 Circle the correct answers.

3) Which TWO words have the long **a** sound?

4) Which TWO words have the long **a** sound?

3RD SOUND OF *a*

Many vowels make a third sound. It is not used as much as the short and long sounds.

 **Listen to the words with the third sound of *a*.**

 **Circle the correct answers.**

5) Which TWO words have the third sound of *a*?

6) Which TWO words have the third sound of *a*?

 **Listen to and write the phonogram.**

SCORE　CORRECT　RESCORE

3. WHAT DO **s**, **d**, AND **m** SAY?

Learn:

- Write and say the sounds for letters **s**, **d**, and **m**.

- Read closed syllables.

Vocabulary:

closed syllable *[klōsd ˊsĭ lŭ bŭl]* – a syllable that ends with a consonant and has one vowel letter that makes its short sound

Listen and review. Mark ⊠ when done.

soup   cheese

Write and say the sounds.

s   s   s   s   s   s

s   •   •   •   •   •

16

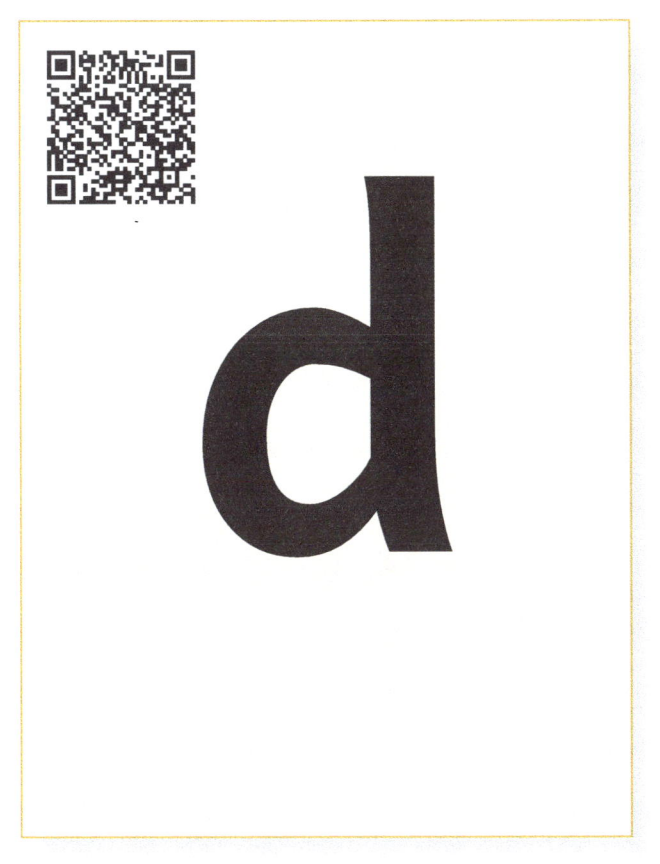

duck   pon**d**

✏️ **Write and say the sound.**

d

d

mint   gu**m**

m

m

 **Circle the correct answers.**

1) Which TWO words begin with **s**?

2) Which TWO words begin with **d**?

3) Which TWO words begin with **m**?

WORKING WITH WORDS

There are different types of syllables. Knowing them helps us read and spell. In this Unit, you will learn how to read closed syllables.

Reading Rules

Closed Syllables: A **closed syllable** has one vowel letter and ends with one or more consonants. The vowel sound is short.

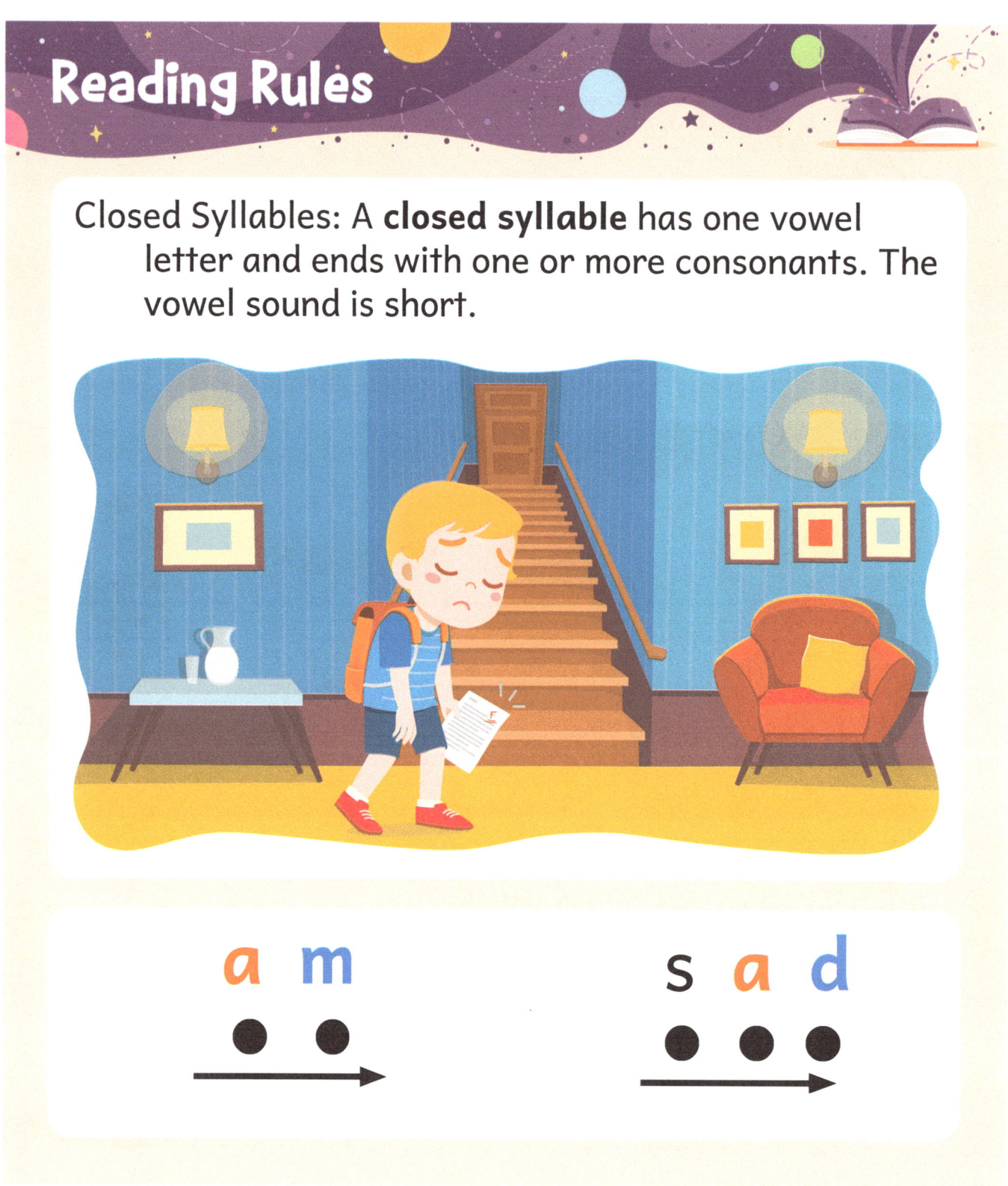

 **Read, write, and circle the correct answers.**

Read	Write	Circle

4) dad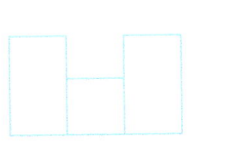

5) ad

6) mad

WRITING PHONOGRAM REVIEW

 **Listen to and write the phonograms.**

PHONOGRAM REVIEW

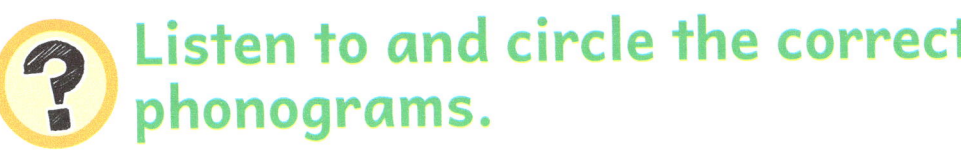

? Listen to and circle the correct phonograms.

1)   a   s   m

2)   s   m   d

3)   d   m   a

4)   a   d   s

SCORE   CORRECT   RESCORE

ACTIVITY: Syllables in Names

Circle the number of syllables in each name.

How many syllables are in your name? ------

Phonogram Test 1

Listen to and write the correct phonograms.

1)

2)

3)

4)

Score _____ 25

4. WHAT DO **i**, **p**, **n**, AND **r** SAY?

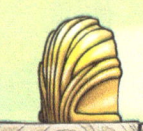

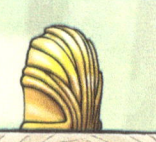

Learn:

- Write and say the sounds for letters **i**, **p**, **n**, and **r**.
- Read words that begin with **s**.

Listen and review. Mark ☒ when done.

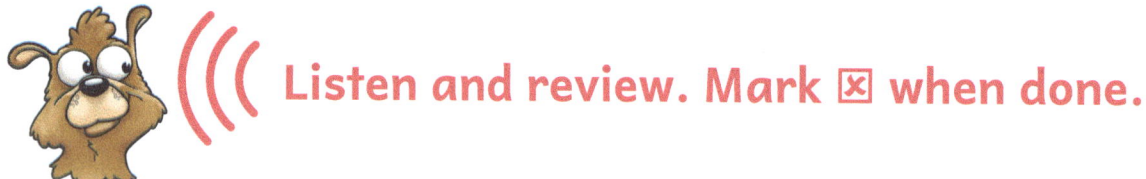

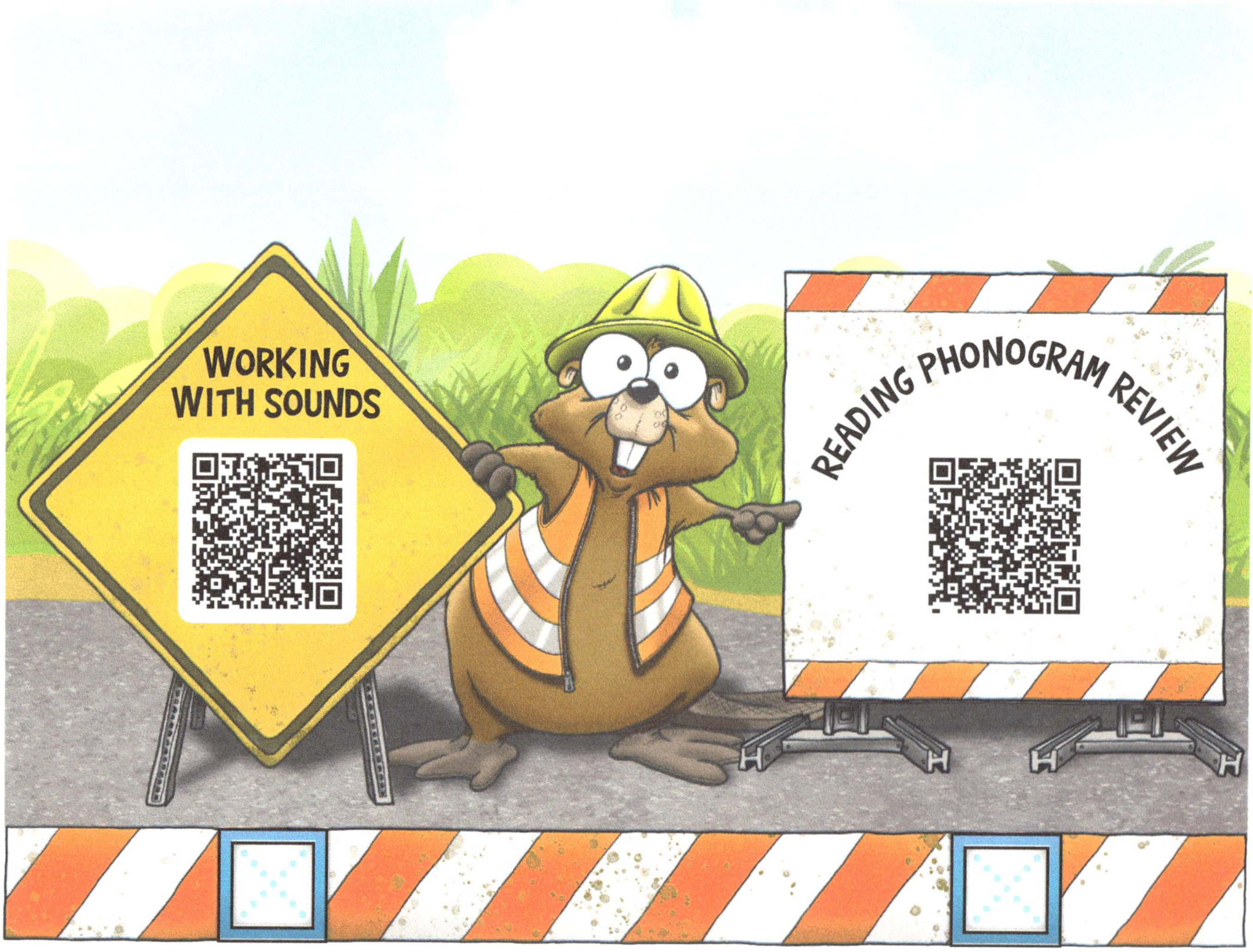

w**i**n   pr**i**ze   chil**i**

✏️ **Write and say the sounds.**

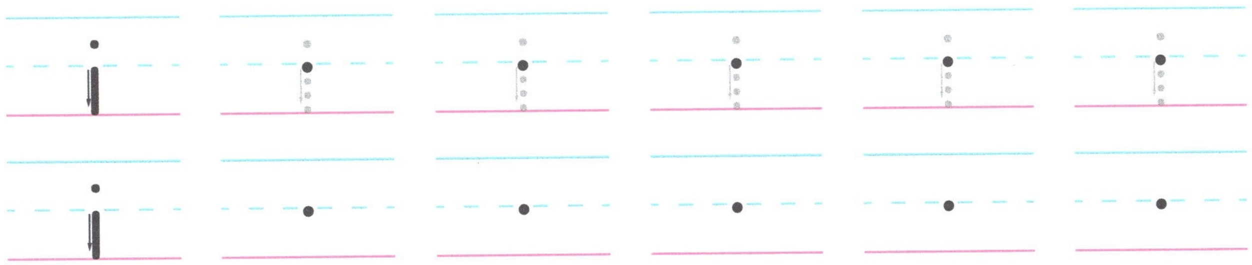

pool   flip

Write and say the sound.

p p

p p

n

new   coi**n**

✏️ **Write and say the sound.**

n   n   n   n   n   n

n   .   .   .   .   .

rice   f**r**y

✏️ **Write and say the sound.**

r   r   r   r   r   r

r

30

 **Circle the correct answers.**

1) Which TWO words have the vowel **i**?

2) Which TWO words begin with **p**?

3) Which TWO words begin with **n**?

4) Which TWO words begin with **r**?

Reading Rules

Beginning **s**: The letter **s** makes its first sound at the beginning of a word.

s a p   s n i p   s p i n

 **Read, write, and circle the correct answers.**

Read	Write	Circle

5) sad

6) snap

7) sip

 **Listen to and write the phonograms.**

SCORE   CORRECT   RESCORE

5. WHAT DO **f**, **o**, **l**, AND **t** SAY?

Learn:

- Write and say the sounds for letters **f**, **o**, **l**, and **t**.

- Read words with double consonants.

Listen and review. Mark ⊠ when done.

fall   scar**f**

✏️ **Write and say the sound.**

f   f   f   f   f   f

f   •   •   •   •   •

36

o

s**o**ft   r**o**be   haird**o**

O   O   O   O   O   O

O   •   •   •   •   •

37

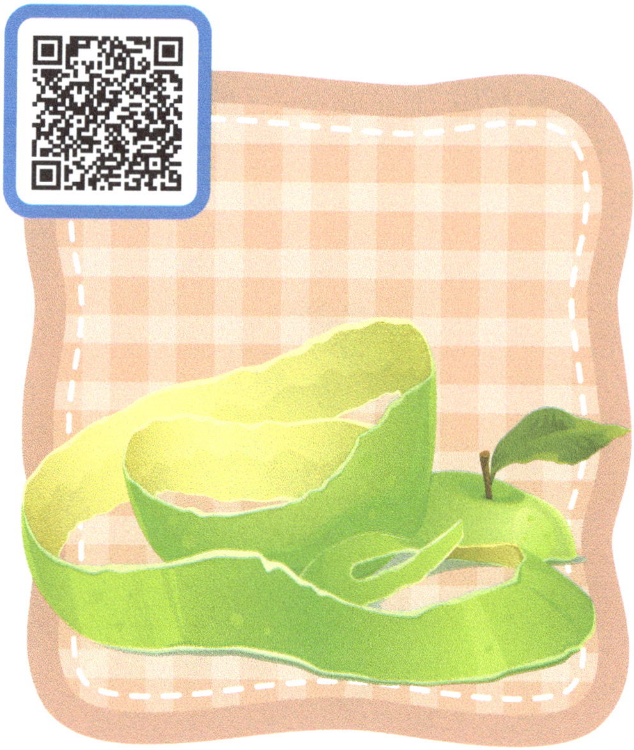

long   pee**l**

✏️ Write and say the sound.

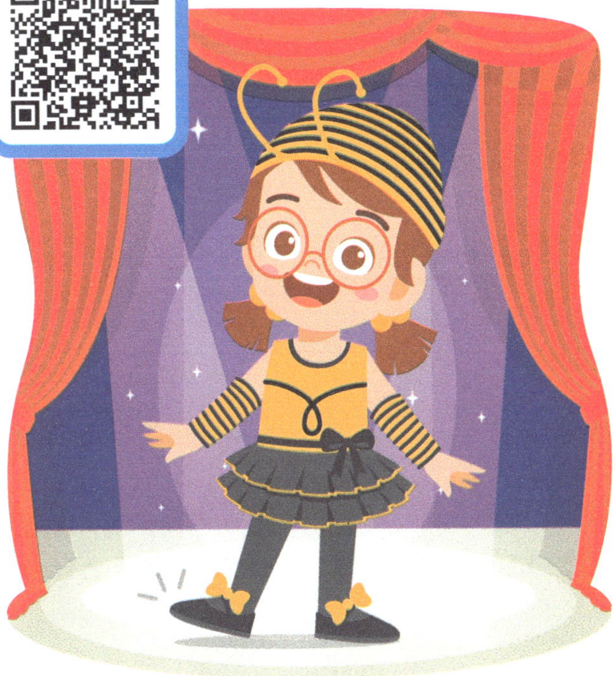

tap   feet

✏️ **Write and say the sound.**

39

 **Circle the correct answers.**

1) Which TWO words begin with **f**?

 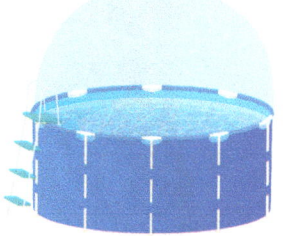  

2) Which TWO words have the vowel **o**?

3) Which TWO words begin with **l**?

4) Which TWO words begin with **t**?

10 2 7 9

Reading Rules

Double consonants: Double consonants usually make one sound.

Double **s**: Double **s** makes the first sound of **s**.

s p i **ll**

p a **ss**

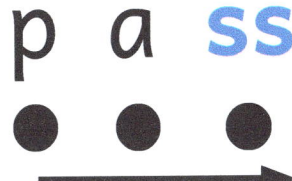

 # Read, write, and circle the correct answers.

Read	Write	Circle
5) fill		
6) sniff		
7) off		
8) toss		

9) doll

10) floss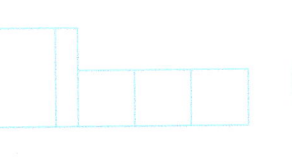

WRITING PHONOGRAM REVIEW

 **Listen to and write the phonograms.**

SCORE   CORRECT   RESCORE

ACTIVITY: Handwriting Practice

Use your best handwriting.

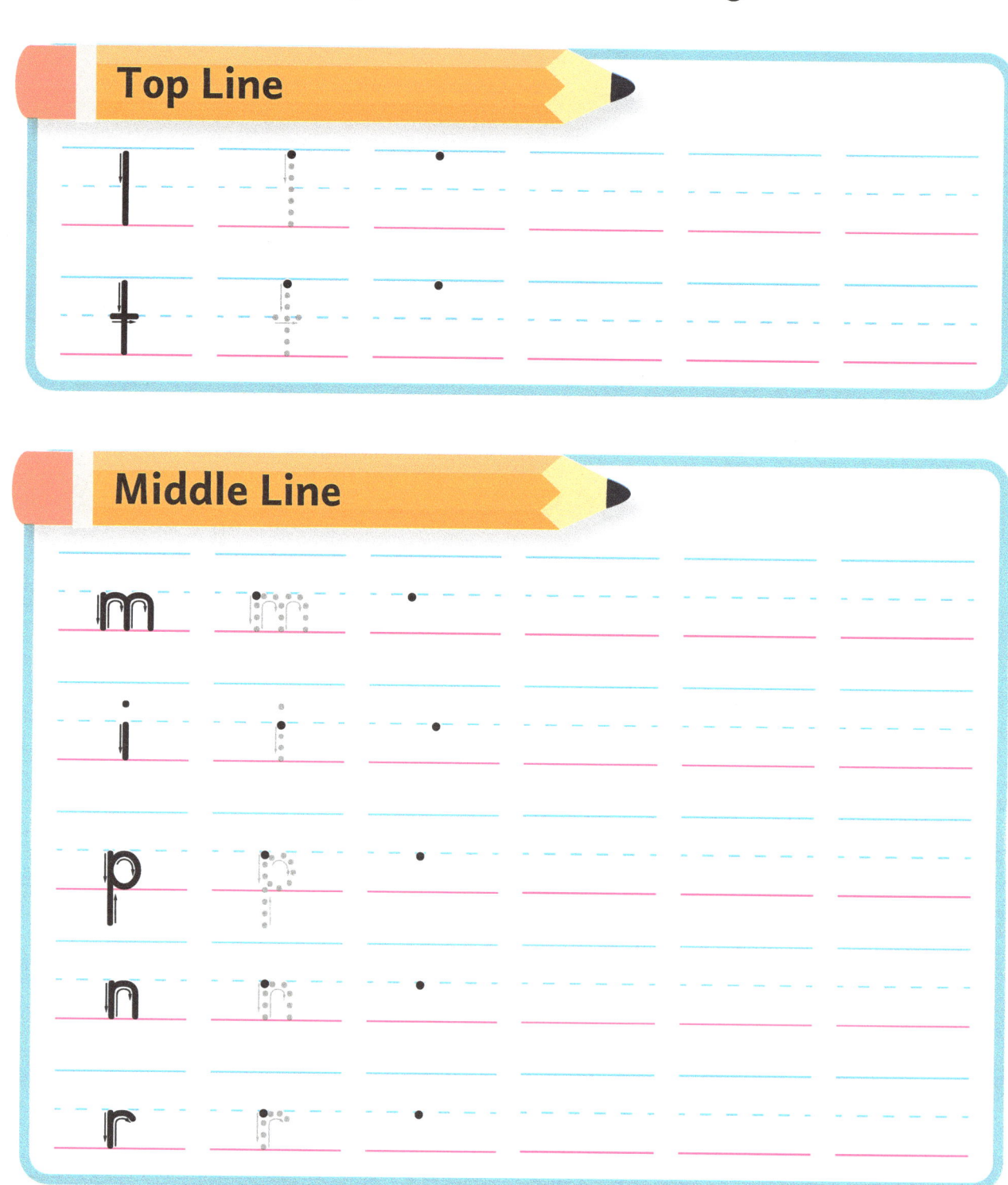

Top Line

l

t

Middle Line

m

i

p

n

r

2 o'clock

a	a				
s	s				
d	d				
f	f				
o	o				

Write *ant, map,* and *ram* under the correct pictures.

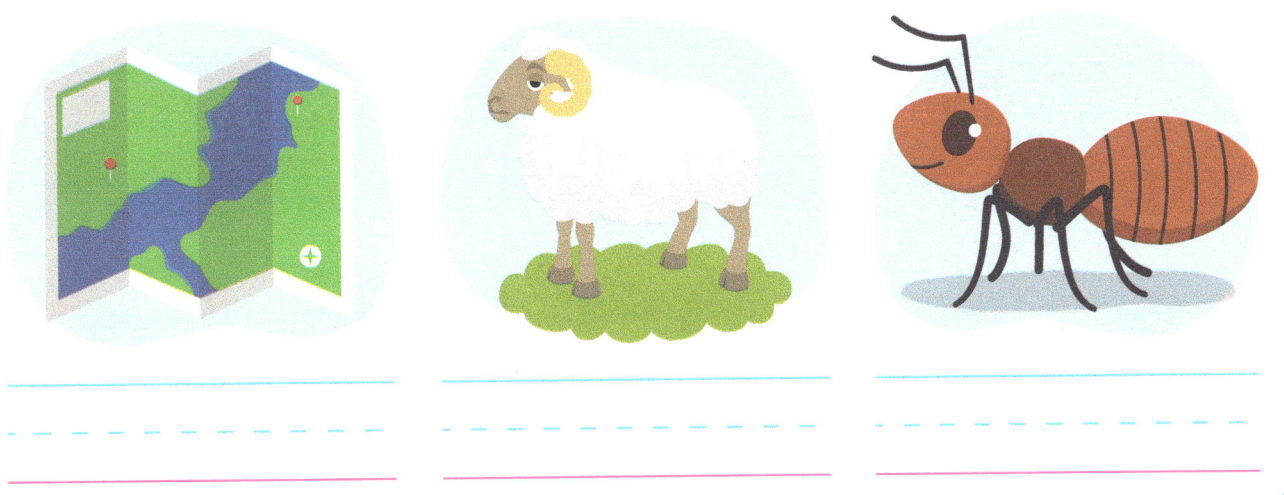

6. WHAT DO **b**, **h**, **u**, AND **w** SAY?

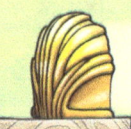

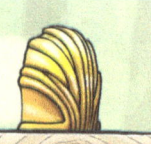

Learn:

- Write and say the sounds for letters **b**, **h**, **u**, and **w**.
- Read words with the third sounds of **a** and **u**.

Listen and review. Mark ☒ when done.

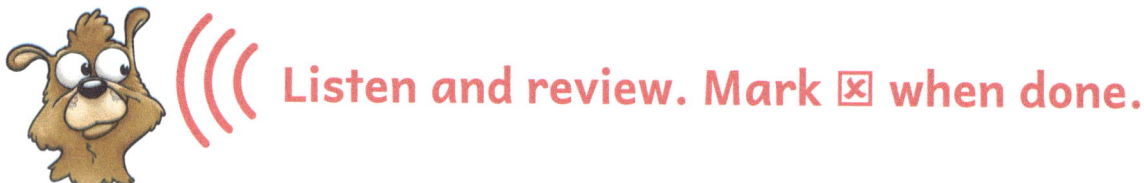

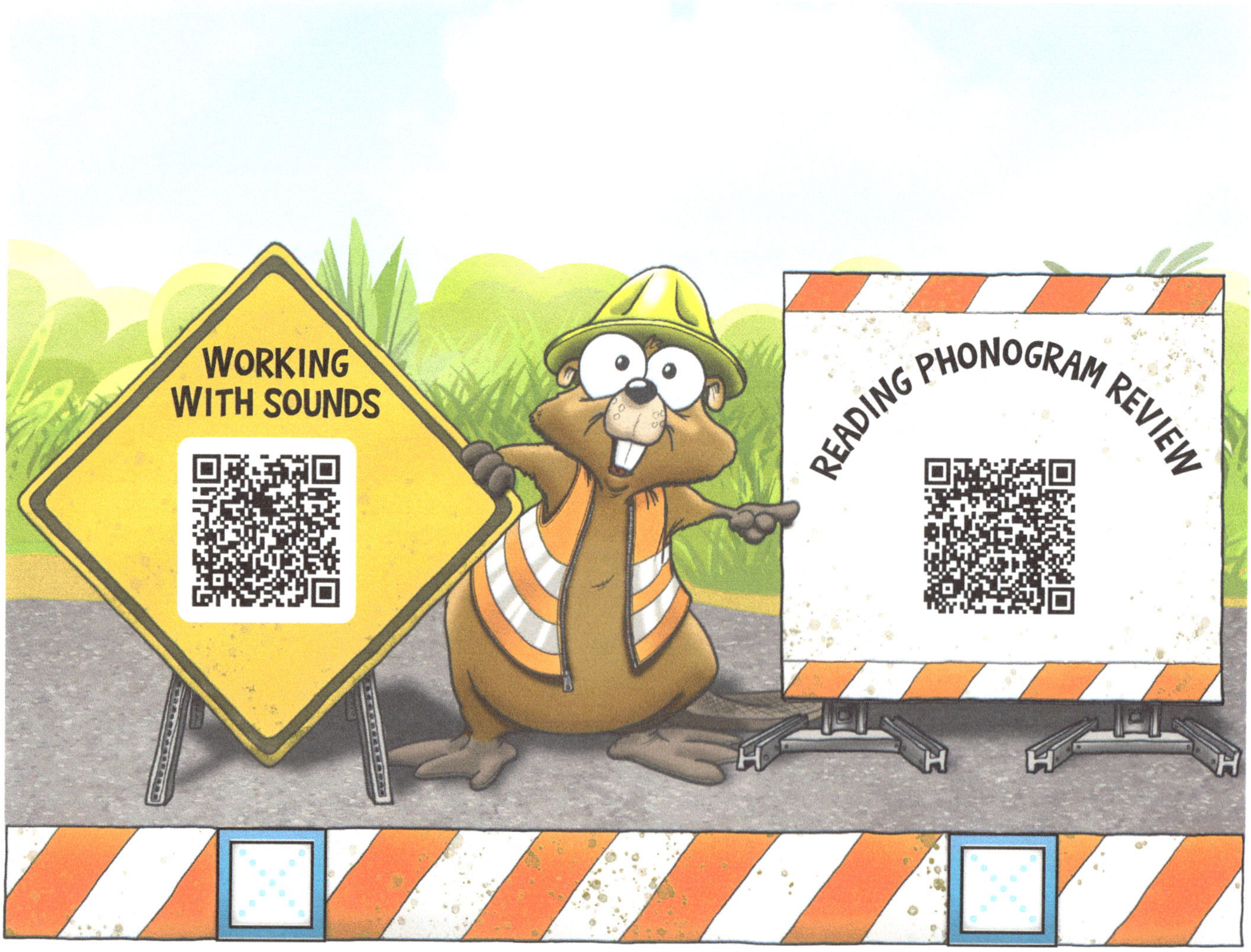

bear   cu**b**

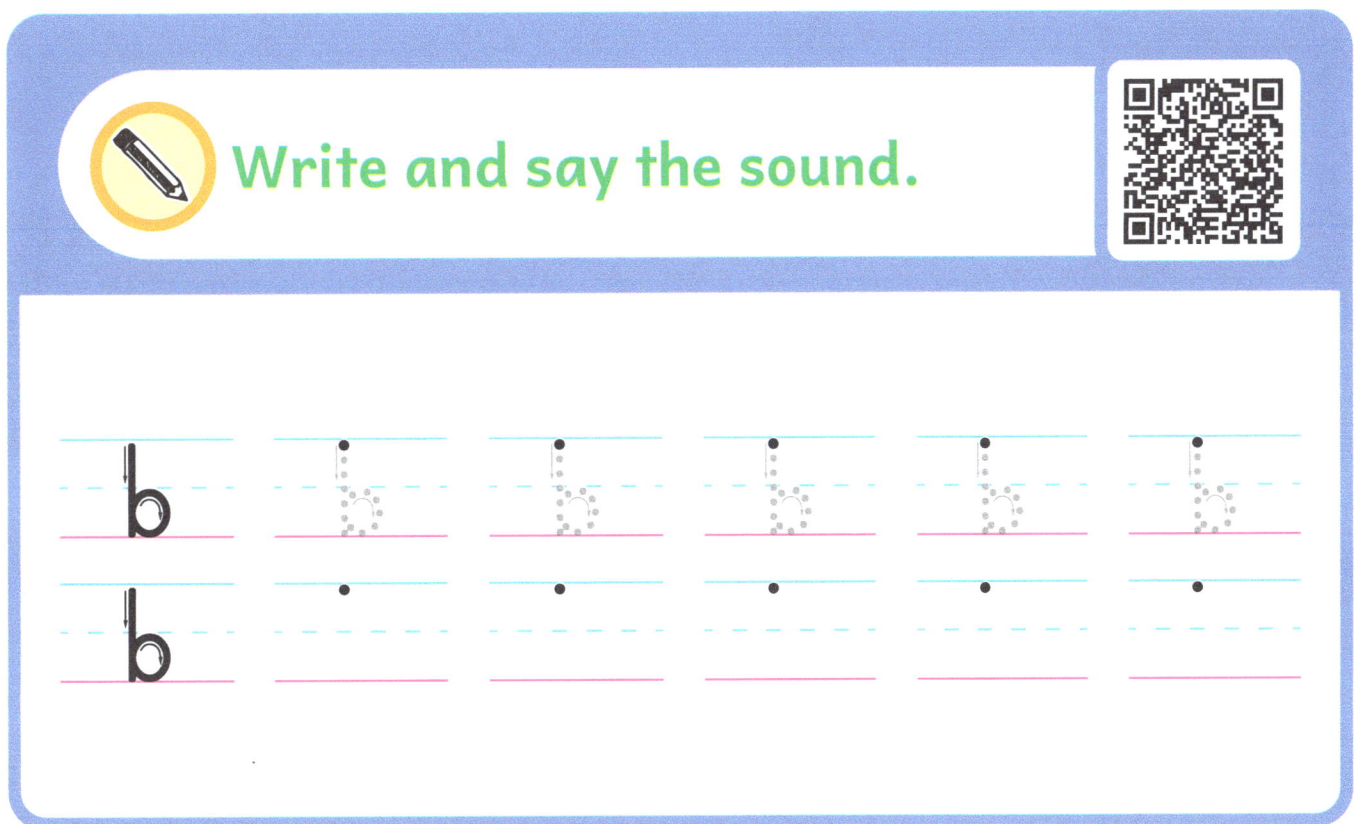

✏️ **Write and say the sound.**

hop   ahead

✏️ **Write and say the sound.**

h h

h

u

p**u**g   c**u**te   p**u**ll

✏️ **Write and say the sounds.**

u   u   u   u   u   u

u

49

wide   a**w**ake

✏️ **Write and say the sound.**

W W W W W W

W

 **Circle the correct answers.**

1) Which TWO words begin with **b**?

  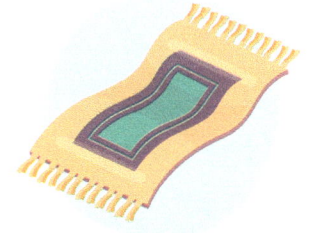 

2) Which TWO words begin with **h**?

3) Which TWO words begin with **u**?

4) Which TWO words begin with **w**?

51

Reading Rules

3rd Sound of **a**: The letter **a** usually makes its third sound after **w** or before **l**.

3rd Sound of **u**: Sometimes, the letter **u** makes its third sound after **p** or **b**. It usually makes its third sound before **l**.

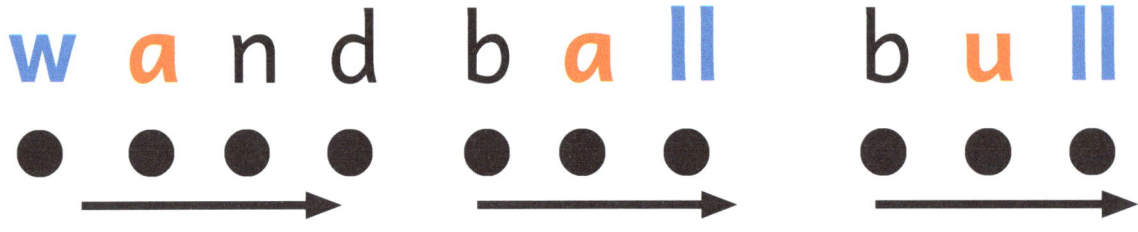

w a n d   b a ll   b u ll

 **Read, write, and circle the correct answers.**

Read	Write	Circle
5) mall		
6) wall		
7) swan		
8) pull		

53

9) swap

10) walk

WRITING PHONOGRAM REVIEW

✏️ **Listen to and write the phonograms.**

SCORE   CORRECT   RESCORE

PHONOGRAM REVIEW

 Listen to and circle the correct phonograms.

1)  b   h   t

2)  u   i   a

3)  f   t   d

4)  m   n   r

5)  i   o   a

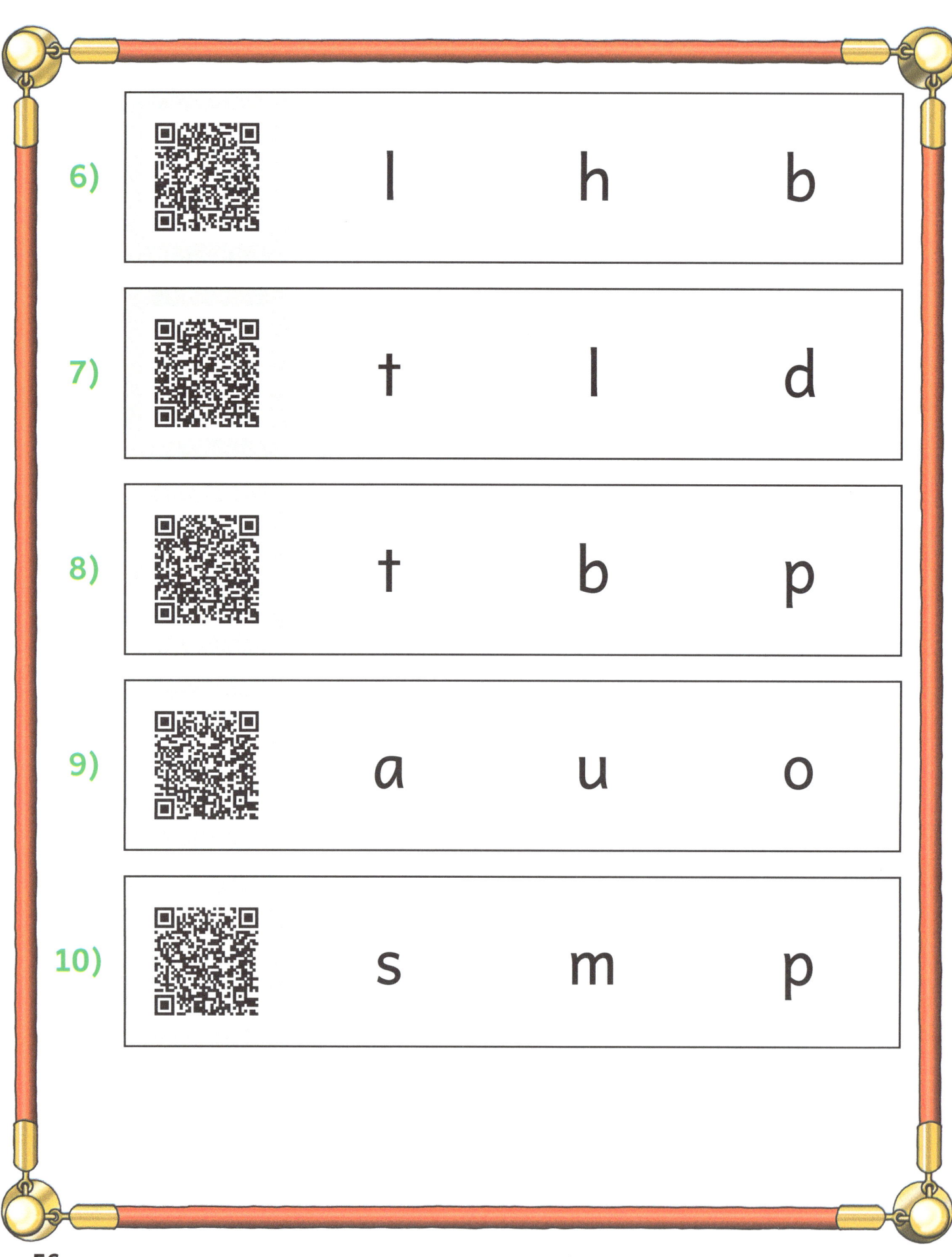

6) l   h   b

7) t   l   d

8) t   b   p

9) a   u   o

10) s   m   p

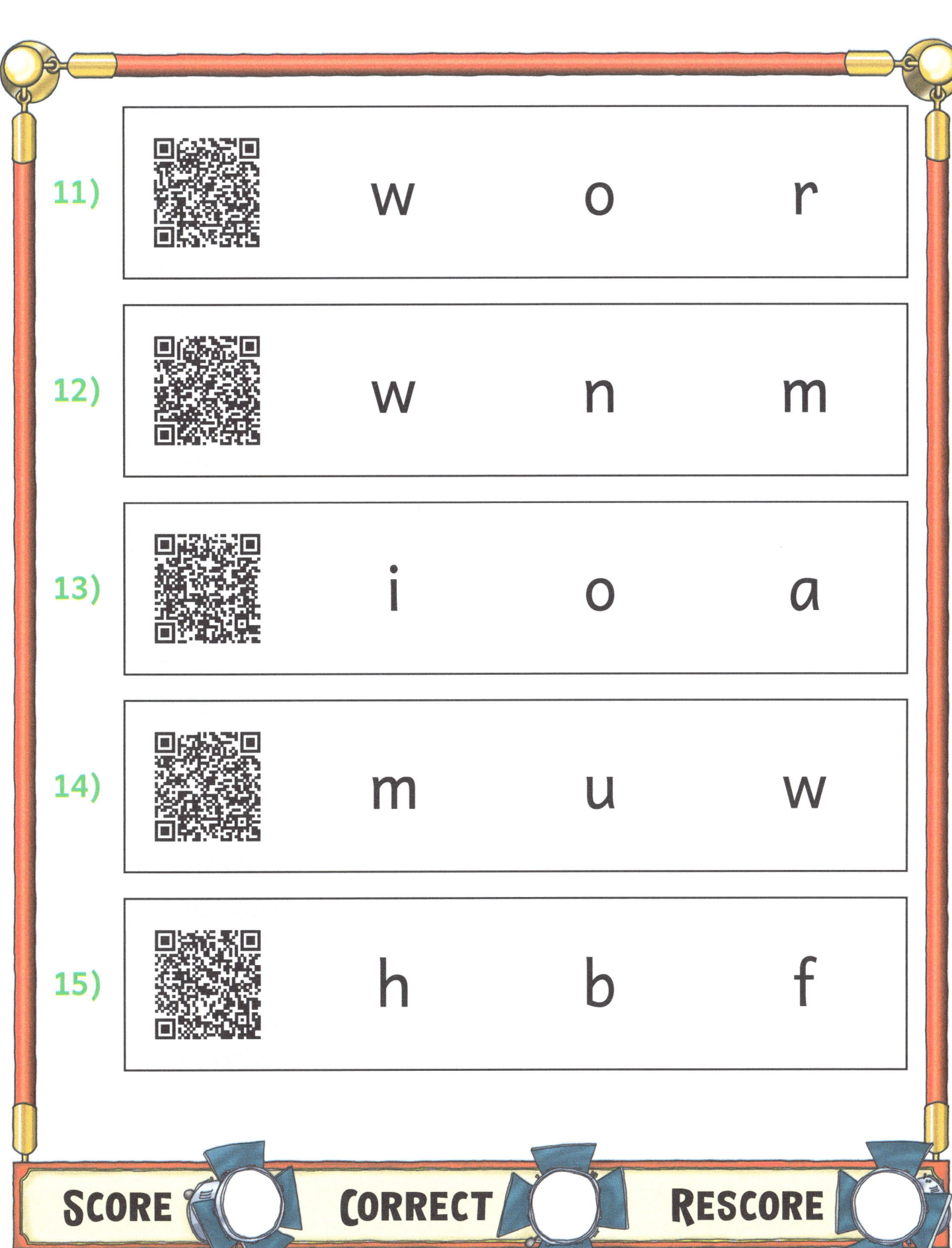

11) w   o   r

12) w   n   m

13) i   o   a

14) m   u   w

15) h   b   f

SCORE   CORRECT   RESCORE

3rd Sound of **a**

sm**all** **wa**sp

3rd Sound of **u**

p**u**t b**u**lb

Write the words under the correct pictures.

swab	tall	full
palm	salt	bull

_____

- - - - - - - - - - - -

_____

_____

- - - - - - - - - - - -

_____

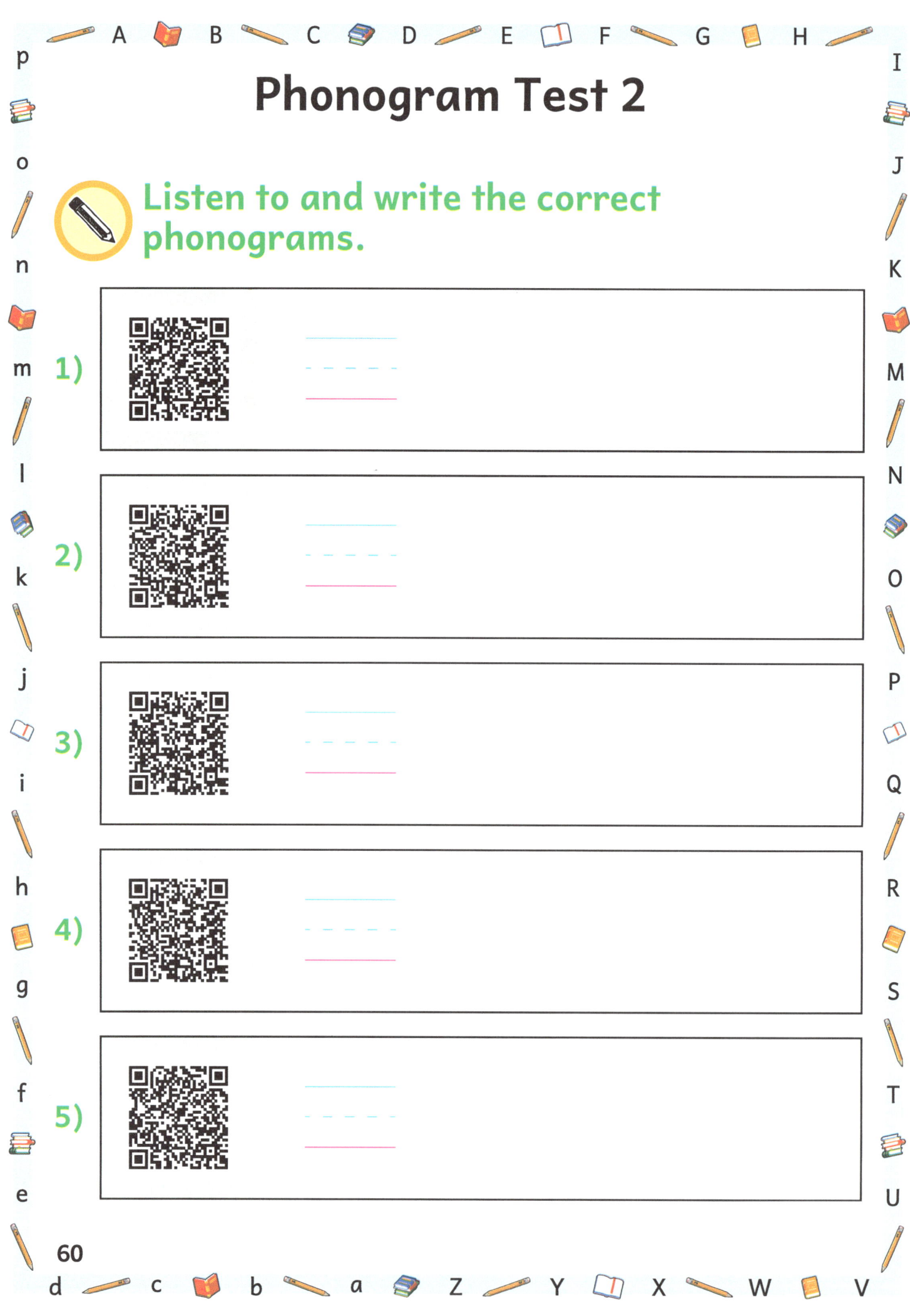

Phonogram Test 2

Listen to and write the correct phonograms.

1)

2)

3)

4)

5)

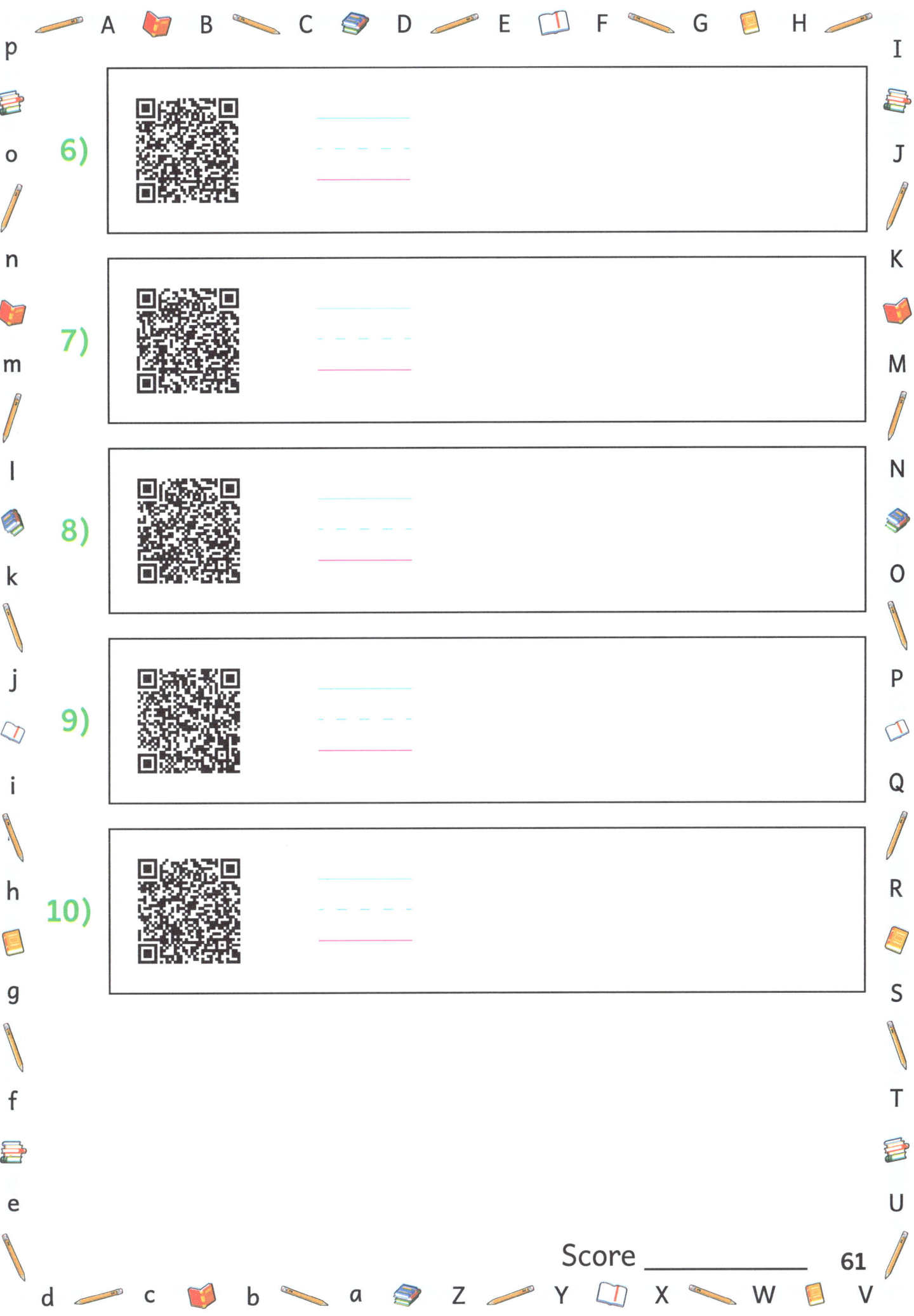

7. WHAT DO **c**, **g**, AND **e** SAY?

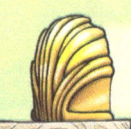

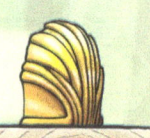

Learn:

- Write and say the sounds for letters **c**, **g**, and **e**.
- Read words with the first sounds of **c** and **g**.

Listen and review. Mark ☒ when done.

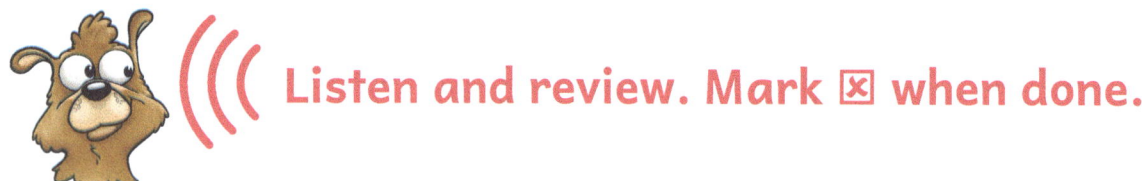

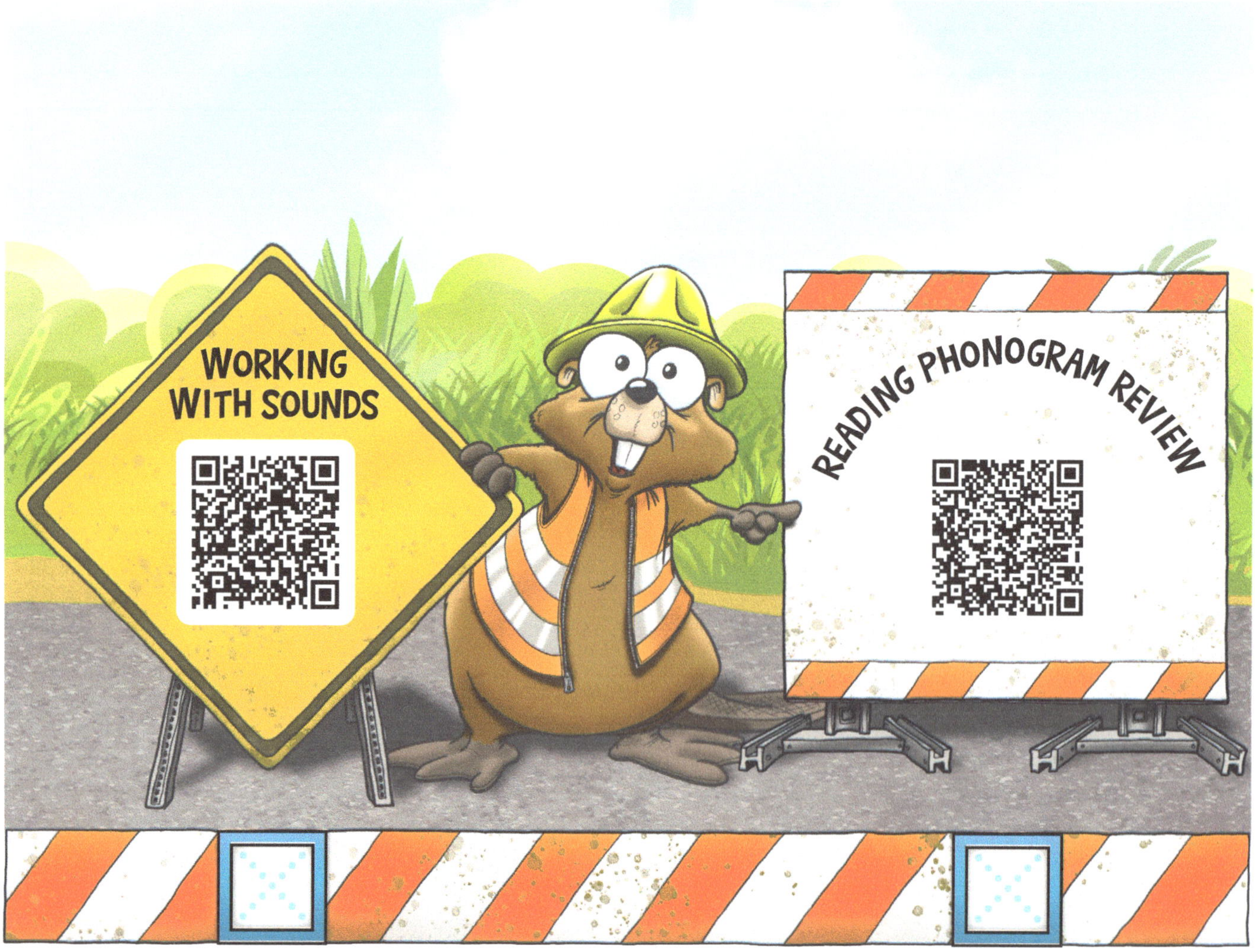

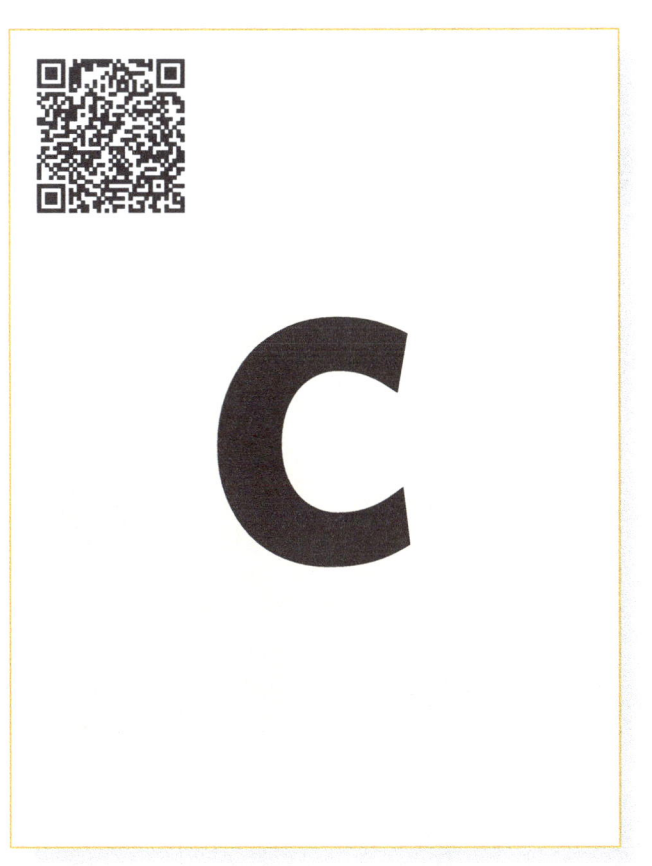

cool   celery

✏️ **Write and say the sounds.**

c

c

63

gold   ca**g**e

Write and say the sounds.

g
g

t**e**n   **e**ven

✏️ **Write and say the sounds.**

e   e   e   e   e   e

e   ·   ·   ·   ·   ·

 **Circle the correct answers.**

1) Which TWO words begin with **c**?

2) Which TWO words begin with **g**?

3) Which TWO words begin with **e**?

66

WORKING WITH WORDS

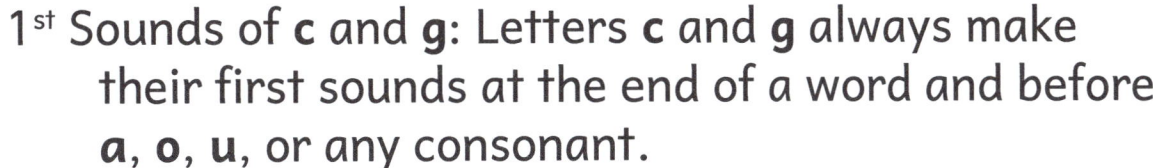

Reading Rules

1ˢᵗ Sounds of **c** and **g**: Letters **c** and **g** always make their first sounds at the end of a word and before **a**, **o**, **u**, or any consonant.

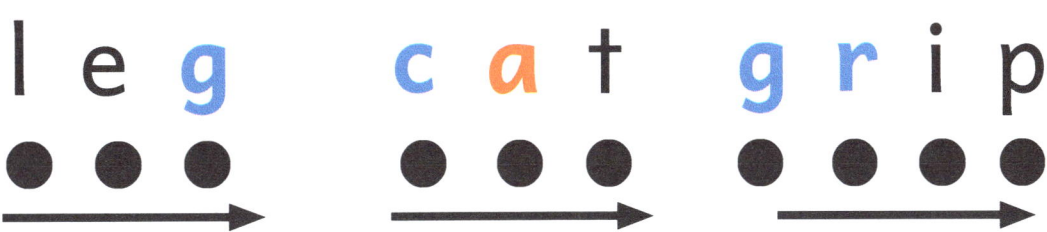

l e **g**   **c** **a** t   **g** **r** i p

 # Read, write, and circle the correct answers.

Read	Write	Circle
4) cup		
5) tag		
6) bag		
7) crab		

68

8) clap

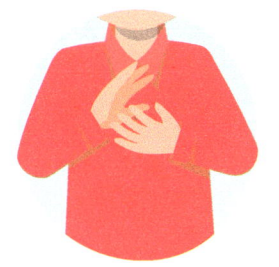 

9) grin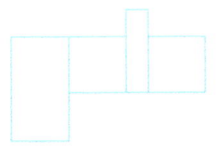

WRITING PHONOGRAM REVIEW

✏️ **Listen to and write the phonograms.**

SCORE   CORRECT   RESCORE

69

Learn:

- Write and say the sounds for letters **k**, **v**, **z**, and **qu**.

- Read words with **k**, **v**, and **z**.

Vocabulary:

multi-letter phonogram *[mŭl tē ´lĕt er ´fō nĭ grăm]* – a phonogram with two or more letters

Listen and review. Mark ⊠ when done.

s**k**y   haw**k**

✏️ **Write and say the sound.**

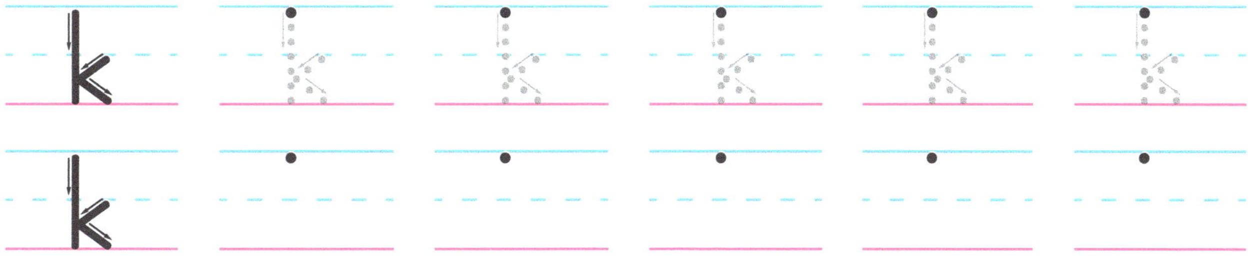

k k k k k k

k k k k k

71

vest   wave

✏️ **Write and say the sound.**

V   V   V   V   V   V

V   V   V   V   V

Z

zoom   whi**z**

✏️ Write and say the sound.

Z z

Z z

The letter **q** is always followed by the letter **u**. It is a multi-letter phonogram. A **multi-letter phonogram** has two or more letters.

s**qu**are **qu**ilt

We underline multi-letter phonograms. This helps us remember that the letters work together.

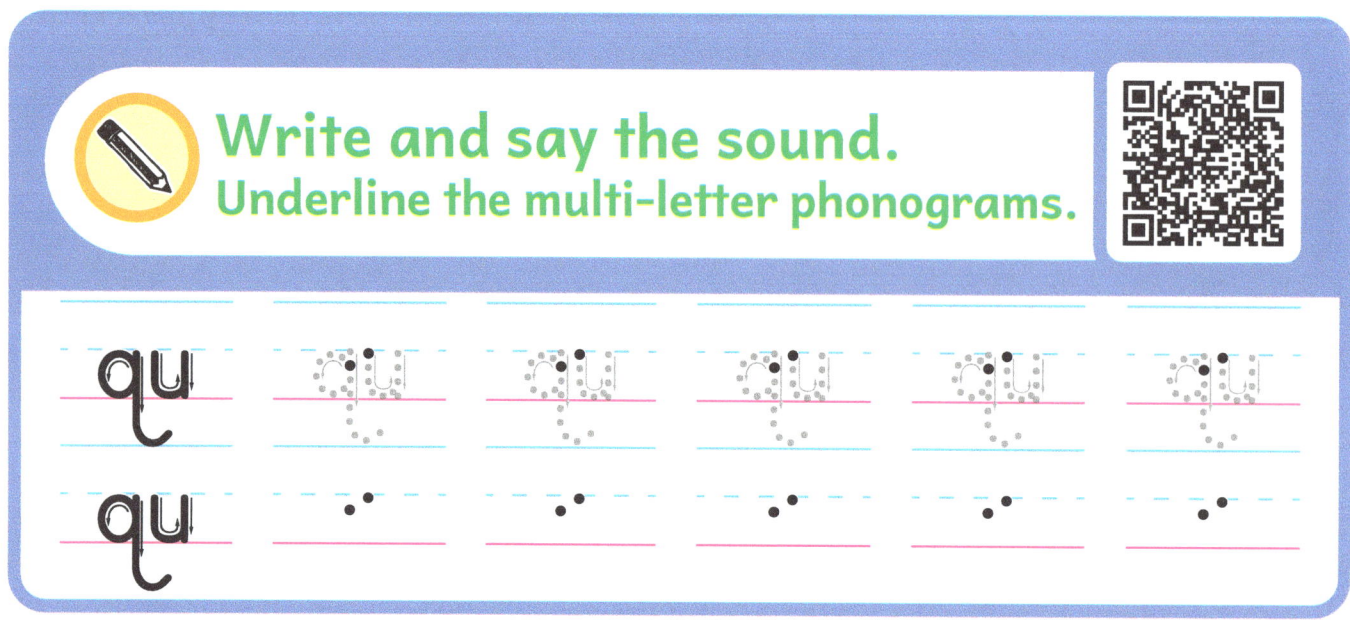

Write and say the sound.
Underline the multi-letter phonograms.

 **Circle the correct answers.**

1) Which TWO words begin with **k**?

2) Which TWO words begin with **v**?

3) Which TWO words begin with **z**?

  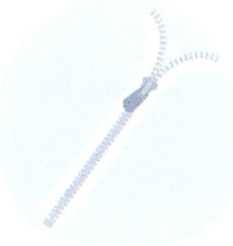 

4) Which TWO words begin with **qu**?

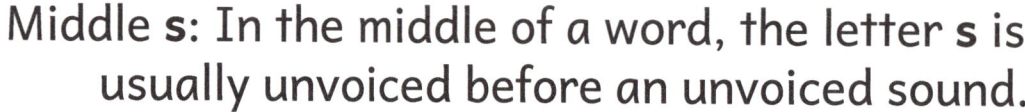

Reading Rules

Middle **s**: In the middle of a word, the letter **s** is usually unvoiced before an unvoiced sound.

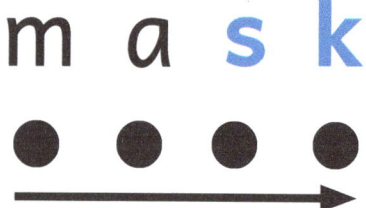

m a s k

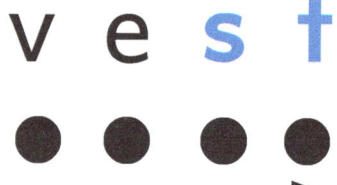

v e s t

 # Read, write, and circle the correct answers.

Read	Write	Circle
5) van		
6) desk		
7) vet		
8) buzz		
9) ask		

10) zip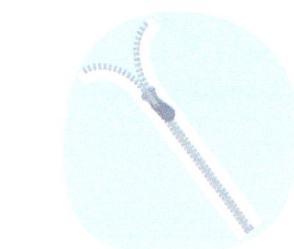

WRITING PHONOGRAM REVIEW

✏️ **Listen to and write the phonograms.**
Underline any multi-letter phonograms.

SCORE **CORRECT** **RESCORE**

ACTIVITY: Reading Rules

Beginning s   **Middle s**   **Double s**

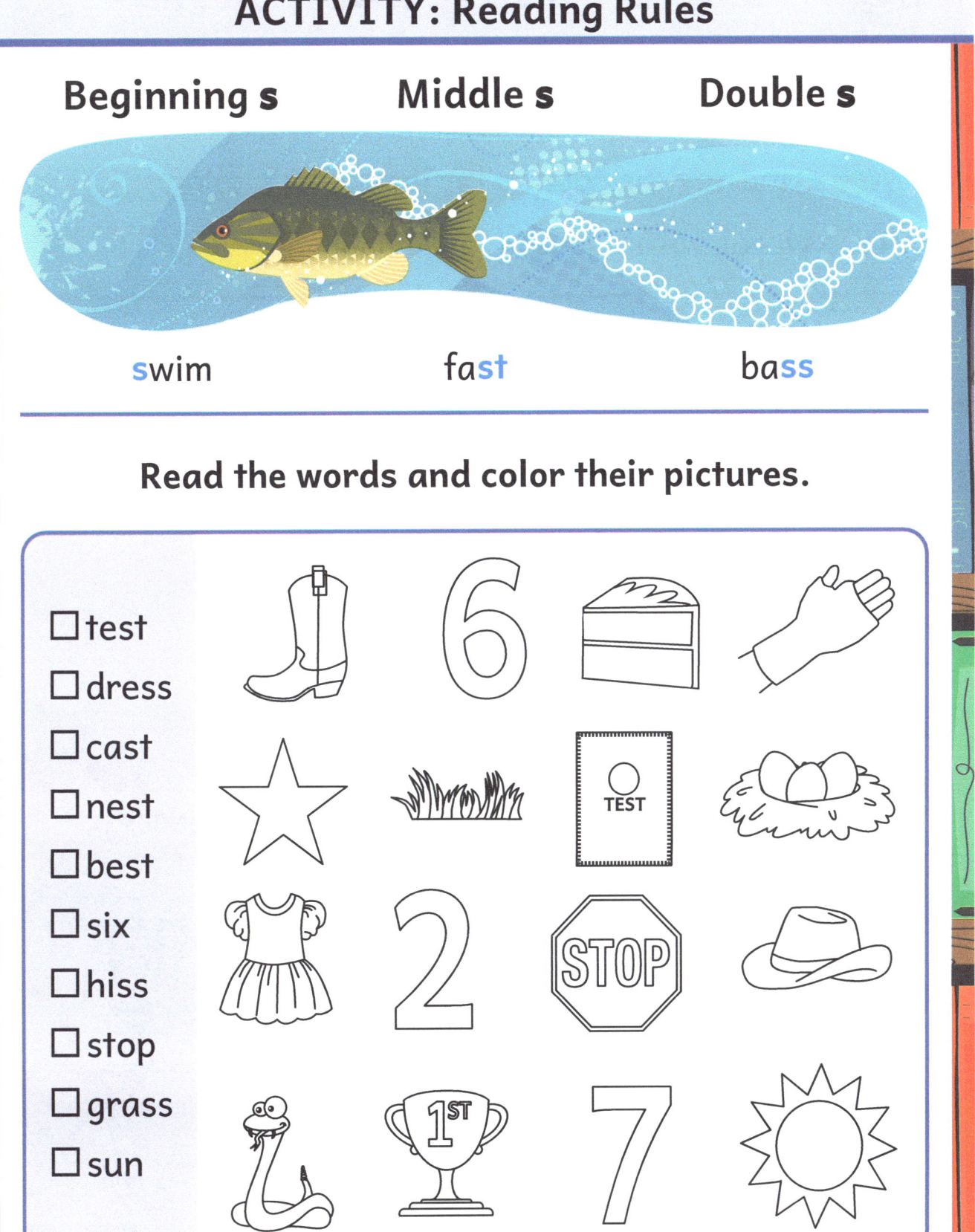

swim   fa**st**   ba**ss**

Read the words and color their pictures.

- ☐ test
- ☐ dress
- ☐ cast
- ☐ nest
- ☐ best
- ☐ six
- ☐ hiss
- ☐ stop
- ☐ grass
- ☐ sun

9. WHAT DO x, j, AND y SAY?

Learn:

- Write and say the sounds for letters **x**, **j**, and **y**.

- Read words with **x**, **j**, and **y**.

🔊 **Listen and review. Mark ☒ when done.**

WORKING WITH SOUNDS

READING PHONOGRAM REVIEW

si**x**   fo**x**es

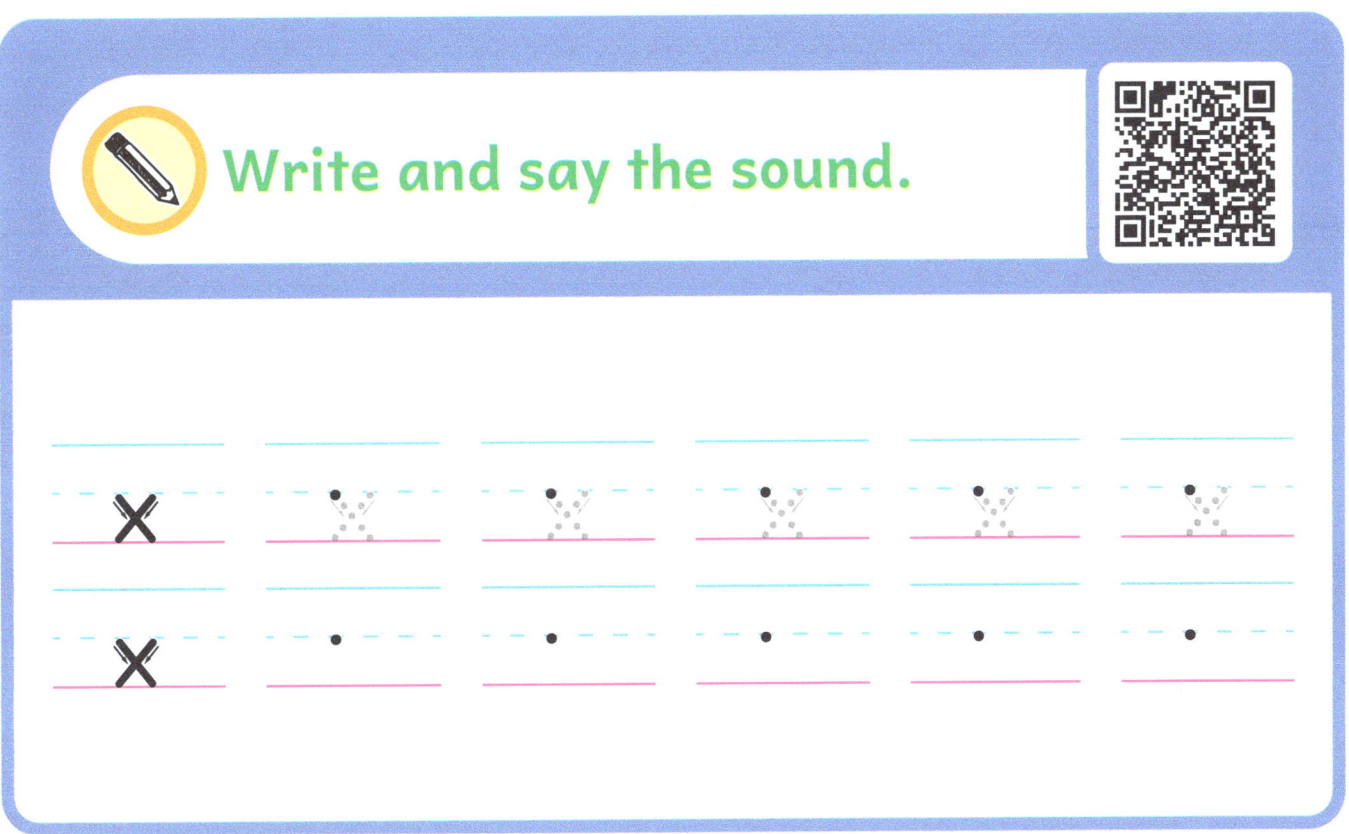

✏️ **Write and say the sound.**

X X X X X X

X

juicy   **j**elly

✏️ **Write and say the sound.**

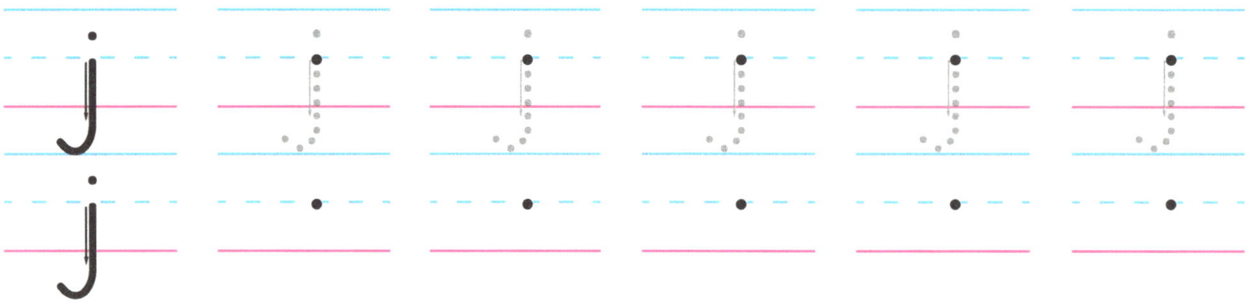

j
j

82

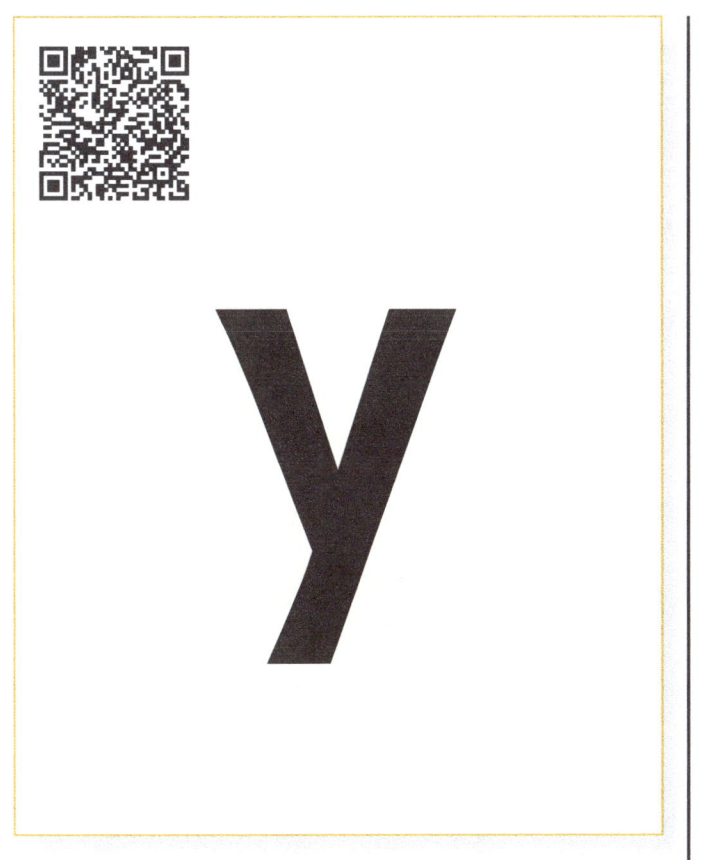

yell   m**y**stery   sp**y**   stor**y**

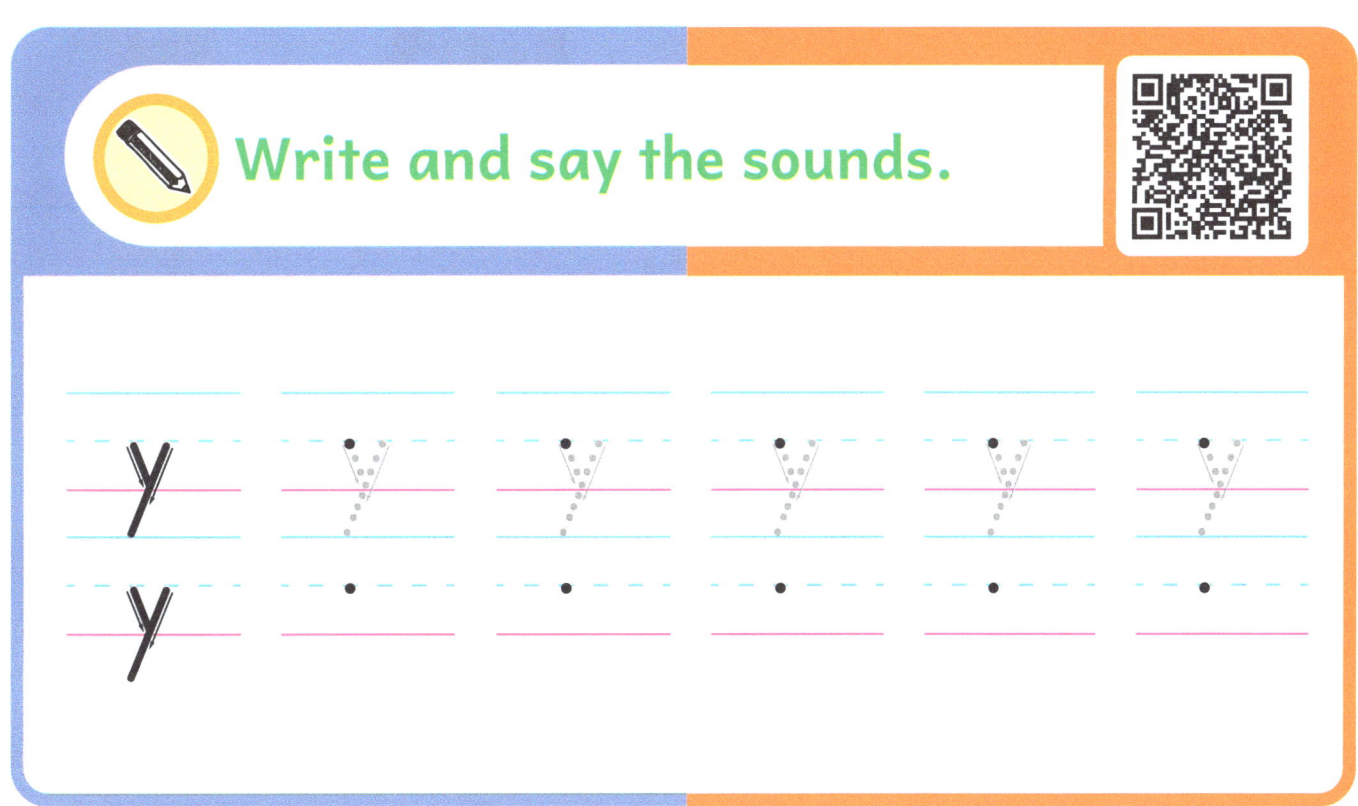

✏️ **Write and say the sounds.**

y y y y y y

y

 **Circle the correct answers.**

1) Which TWO words end with **x**?

2) Which TWO words begin with **j**?

3) Which TWO words begin with **y**?

WORKING WITH WORDS

Reading Rules

Beginning **y**: The letter **y** always makes its consonant sound at the beginning of a word.

y a k

y a m

 **Read, write, and circle the correct answers.**

Read	Write	Circle

4) yell

5) yes

6) jet

7) box

8) fox

9) jug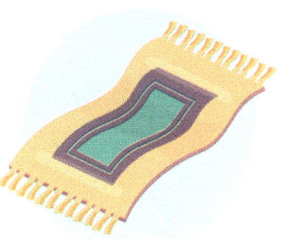

WRITING PHONOGRAM REVIEW

PHONOGRAM REVIEW

 Listen to and circle the correct phonograms.

1)  s   qu   k

2)  w   x   z

3)  r   w   s

4)  a   p   n

5)  i   e   y

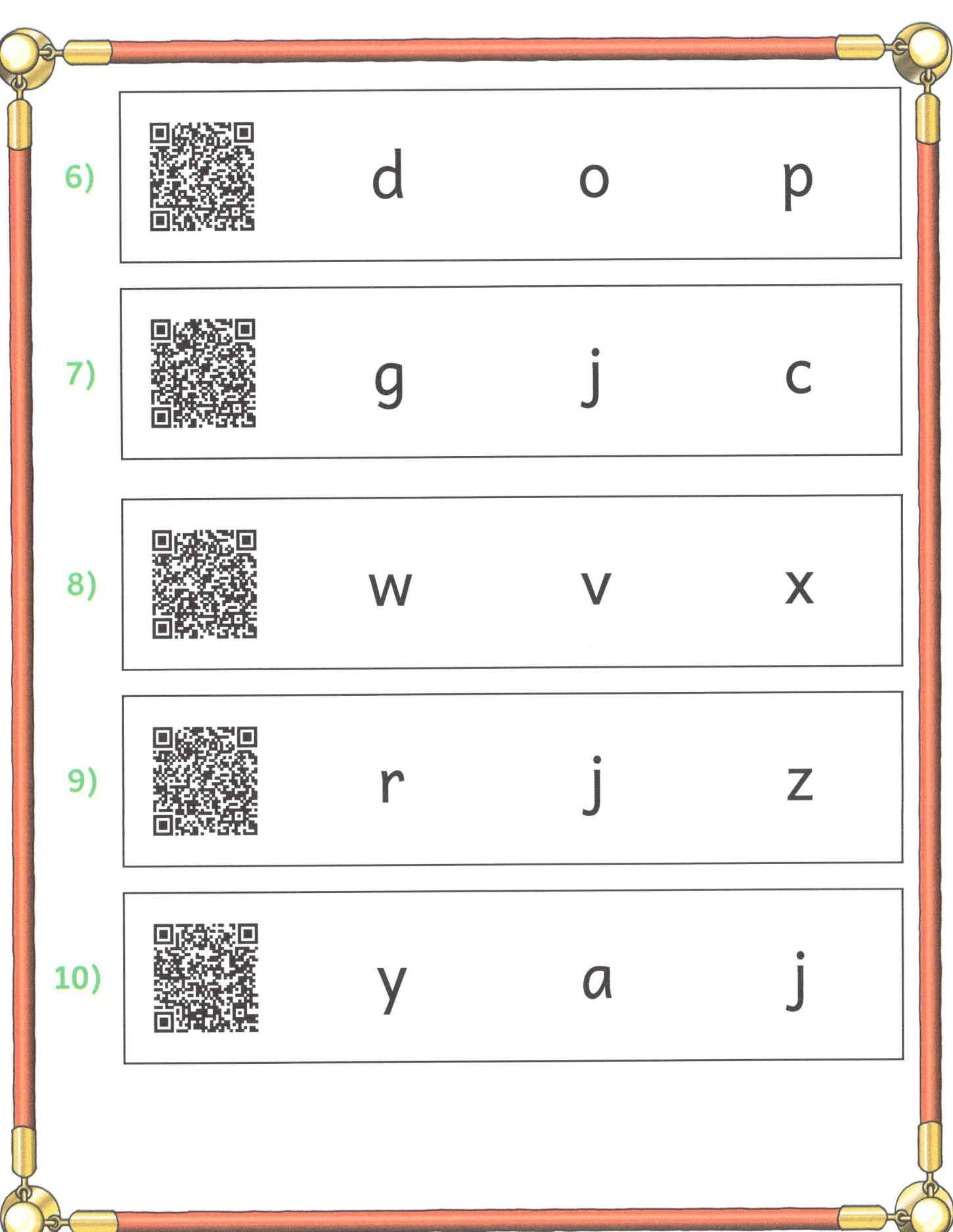

6)   d   o   p

7)   g   j   c

8)   w   v   x

9)   r   j   z

10)   y   a   j

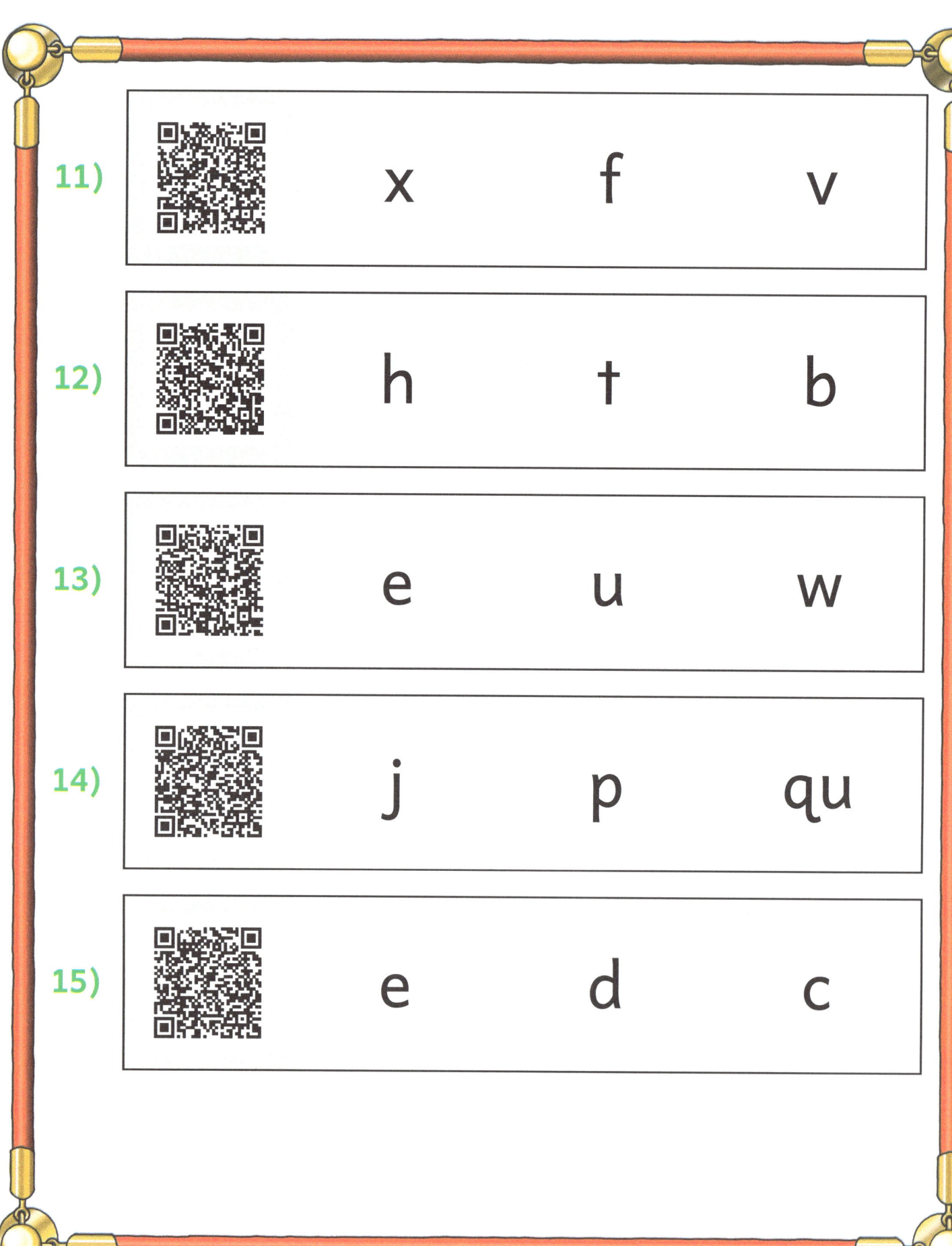

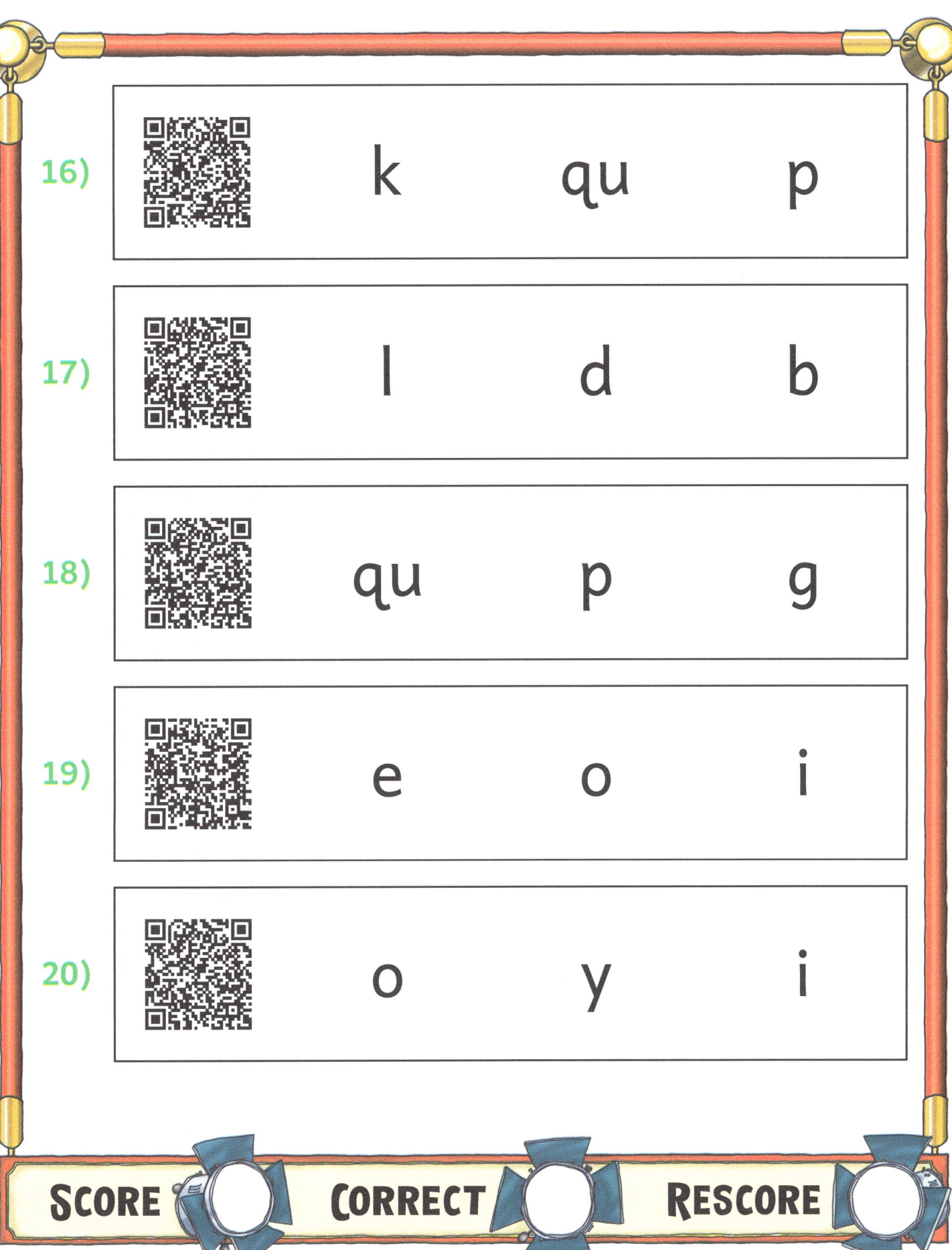

16) k   qu   p

17) l   d   b

18) qu   p   g

19) e   o   i

20) o   y   i

SCORE   CORRECT   RESCORE

ACTIVITY: Handwriting Practice

Use your best handwriting.

Top Line

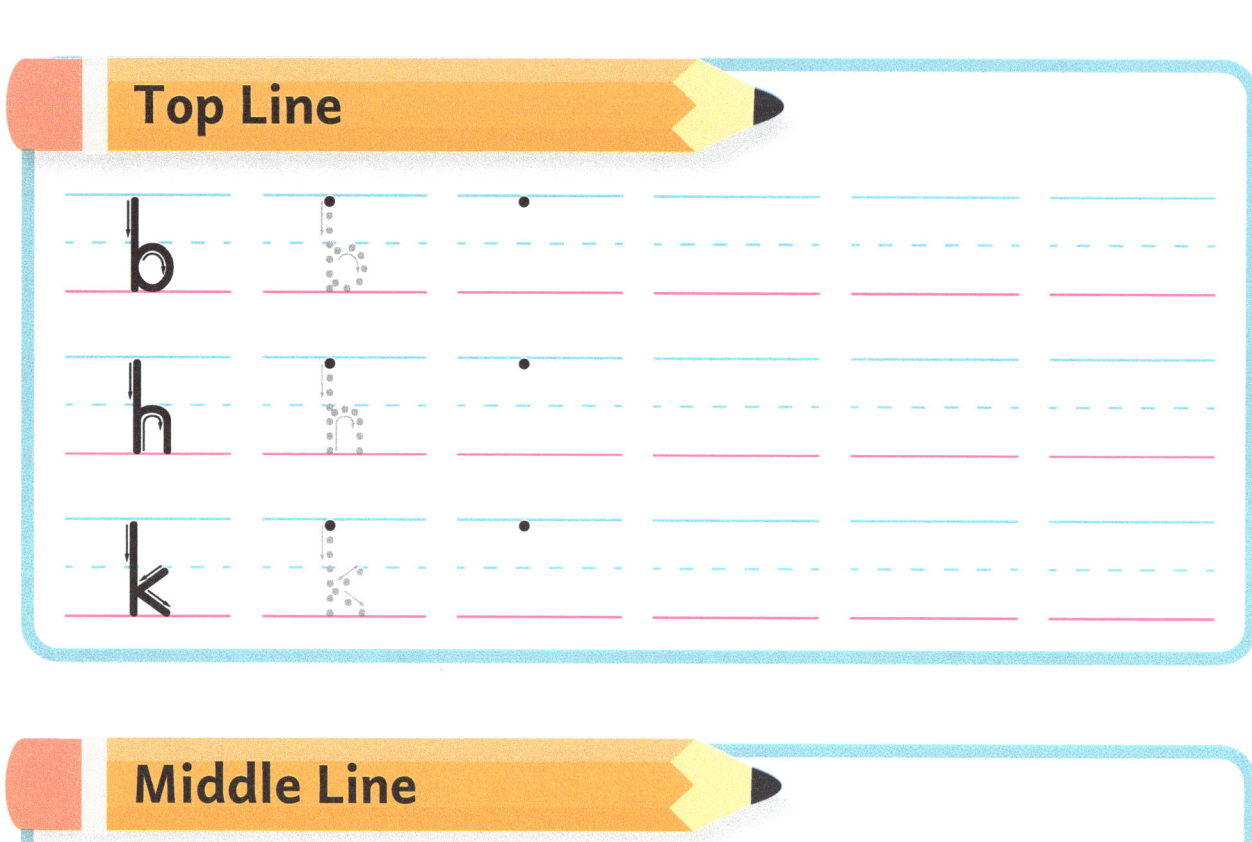

Middle Line

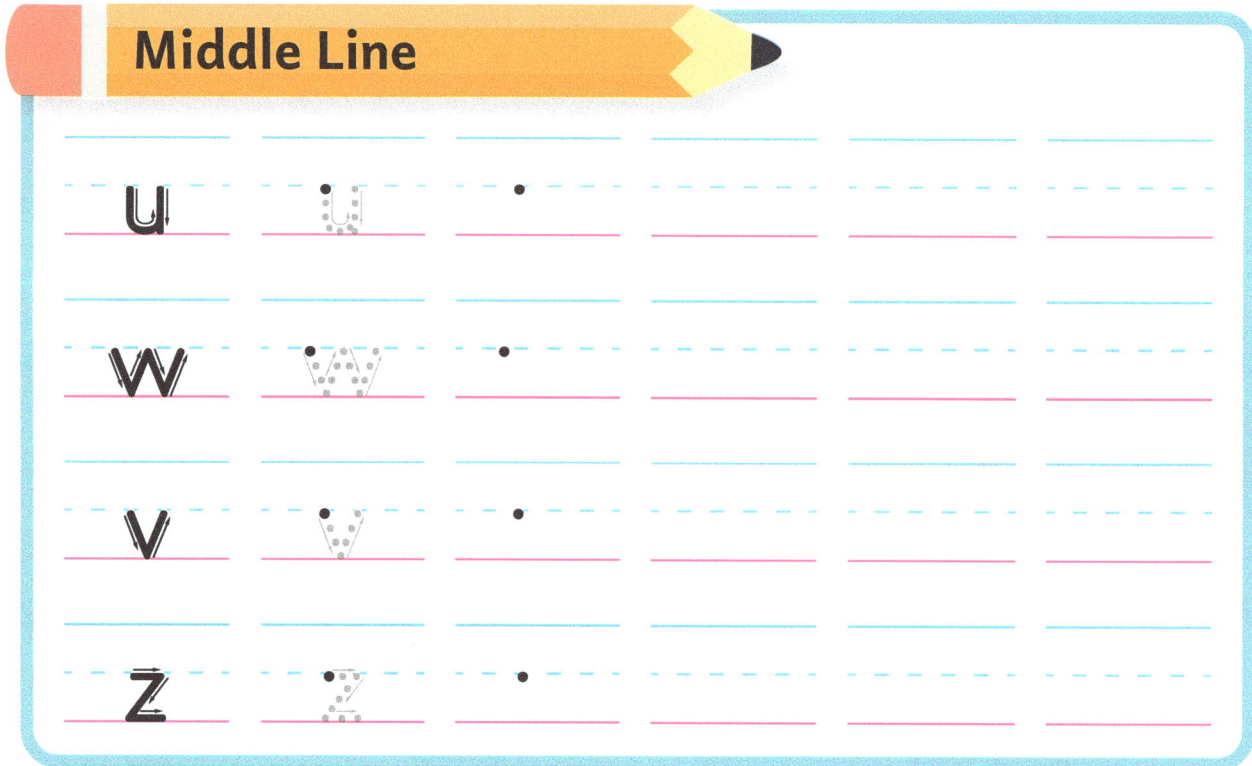

Middle Line *continued*

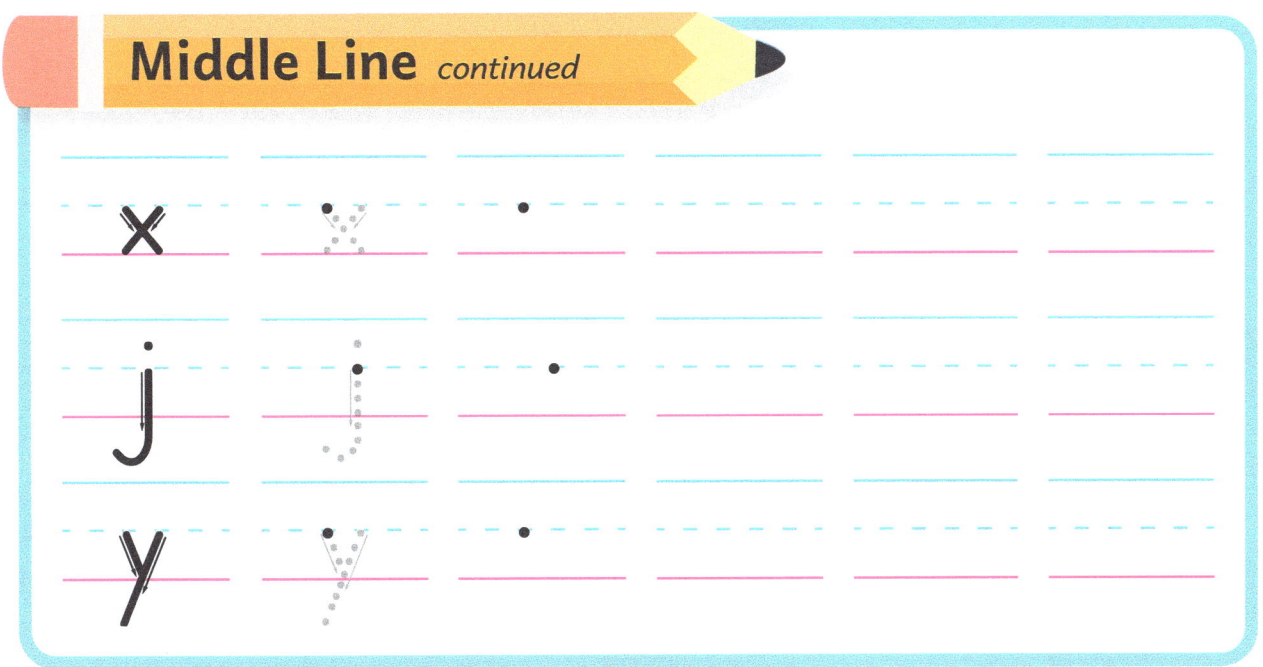

x   y

j   j

y   y

2 o'clock

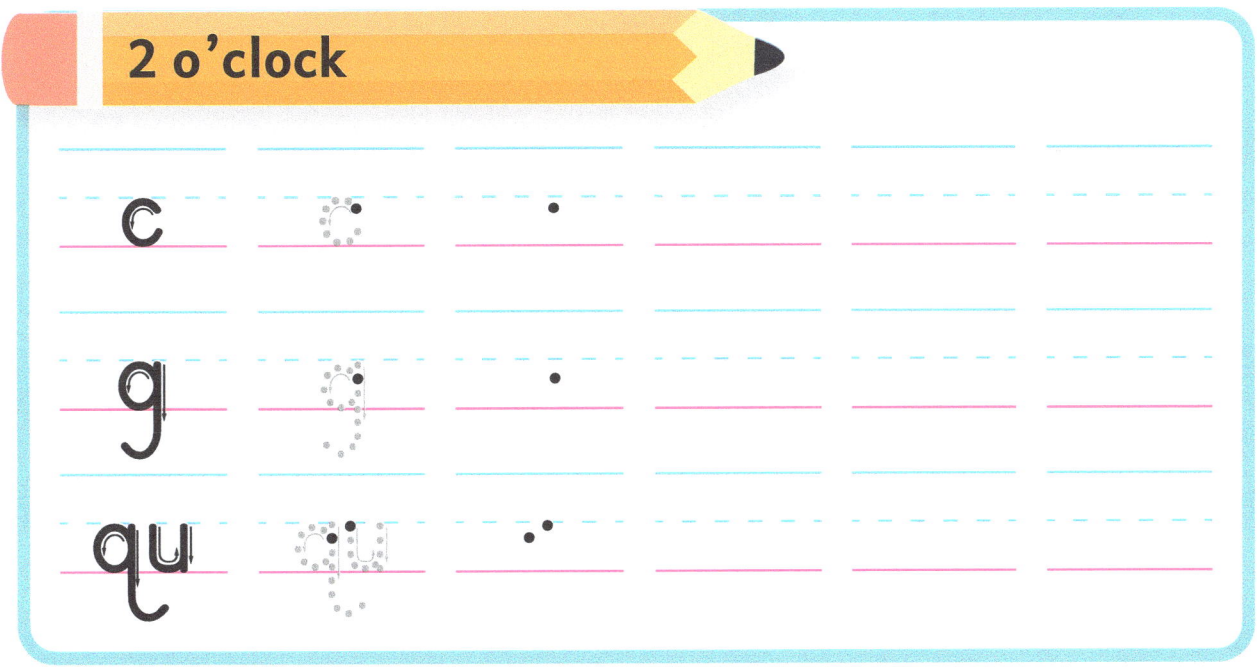

c   c

g   g

qu   qu

10 o'clock

e

Write *bug*, *web*, and *cub* under the correct pictures.

Phonogram Test 3

Listen to and write the correct phonograms.
Underline any multi-letter phonograms.

1)

2)

3)

4)

5)

95

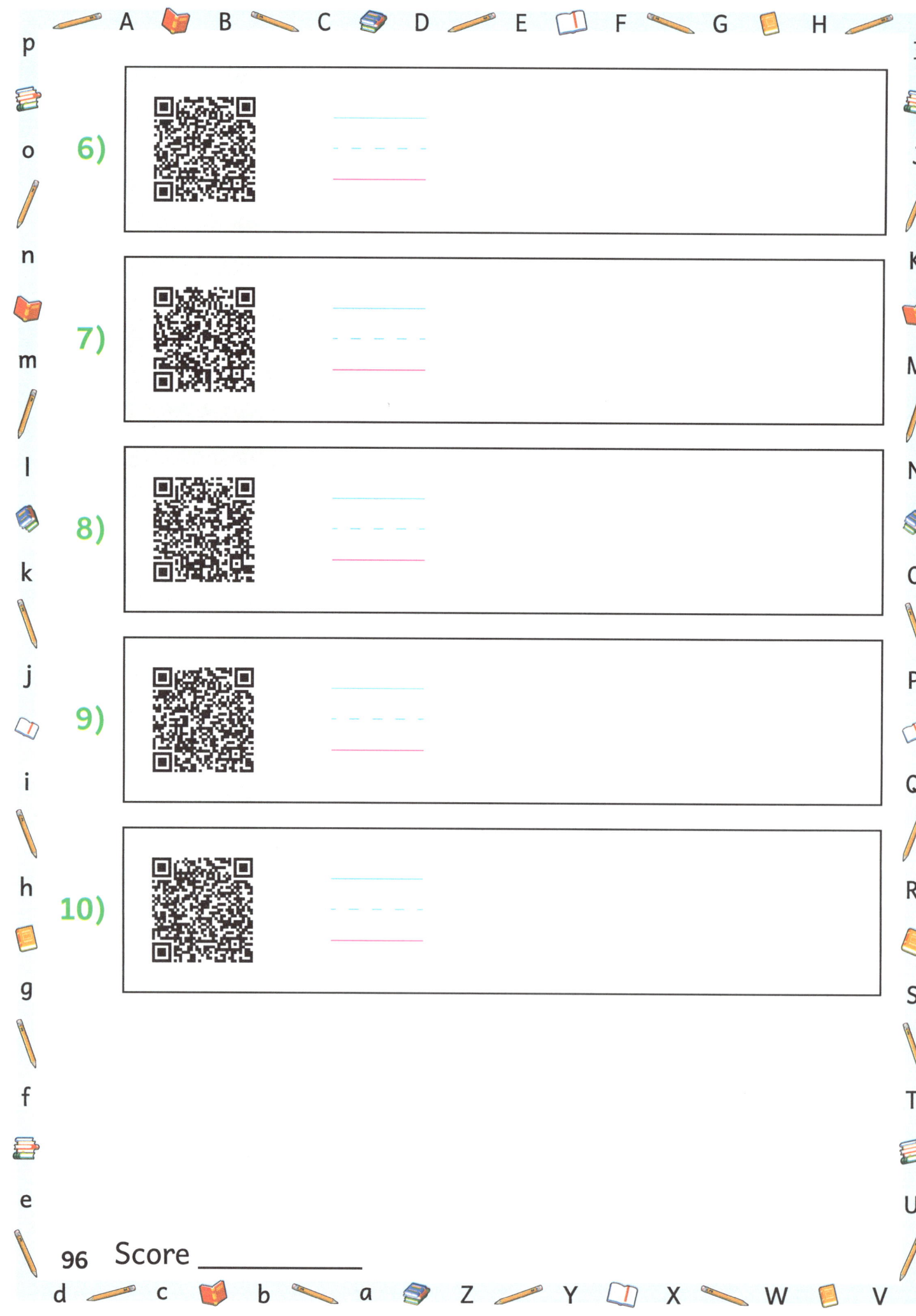

Score _____